WORLD STREET FOOD

EASY RECIPES FOR YOUNG TRAVELLERS

Carolyn Caldicott • Photographs by Chris Caldicott

PIMPERNEL
PRESS LTD
www.pimpernelpress.com

ICI → POISSON FRAIS

Pimpernel Press Limited
www.pimpernelpress.com

World Street Food
© Pimpernel Press Limited 2017
Text © Carolyn Caldicott 2017
Photographs © Chris Caldicott 2017

A catalogue record for this book is available from the British Library.

Designed by Becky Clarke Design
Typeset in Mrs Eaves and My Underwood

ISBN 978-1-910258-39-2
Printed and bound in China
by C&C Offset Printing Company Limited

9 8 7 6 5 4 3 2 1

CONTENTS

INTRODUCTION

This is *the* cookbook to have in your first kitchen away from home. A collection of simple yet innovative travellers' favourites that won't break the bank, *World Street Food* recreates the tantalizing tastes of street stalls and night markets, trattorias and tea-houses, camp-fire cook-ups and comfort food in backpacker cafés. It simplifies on-the-road classics, using ingredients that you don't have to go to the ends of the earth to find and providing clear cooking instructions. Every recipe is versatile, giving vegetarian options where appropriate, as well as tips for those who really want to recreate the authentic street stall flavours.

Be transported to the European tracks with tasty tapas, the teeming streets of India sipping homemade lassi, the heights of Table Mountain munching bunny chow, a late night Latin American bar snacking on avocado completos, or feel the sand between your toes as you savour a fragrant Thai coconut curry . . .

LEFT Chinese fishing nets, Cochin, Kerala

GETTING STARTED

Following the lead of street stalls and cafés, the mantra of this book is to keep it simple. All the recipes are written with the practicalities of a start-up kitchen in mind and aim to keep kitchen equipment to a minimum. The recommended basic kit sticks to indispensable bits and pieces. Anything from the wish list is a bonus — although if you love cooking they might soon become a priority.

Before hitting the shops, you will obviously beg or borrow any useful pots and pans that are gathering dust at home. Charity shops and car boot sales are also worth a rummage, and Asian stores stock a wide range of inexpensive odds and ends, from woks to chopping knives.

LEFT A back-of-the truck street stall in Gallipoli, Italy

KITCHEN KIT

THE BASICS

Wok: The 'must have' cooking pan offers flexible cooking beyond the stir-fry. Think pasta sauce, curries and noodle soups for starters.

Small and large heavy-bottomed frying pans: Non-stick is preferable and a good-quality brand is more durable, assuming it's treated with respect (i.e., avoid abrasive utensils and cleaning products that damage the surface).

Small and medium heavy-bottomed saucepans with lids: If group cooking is on the agenda, club together and add a large saucepan to the list.

Small and medium casserole dishes

Small and medium mixing bowls

Chopping board: It's a good idea to mark one side of the board solely for the preparation of meat.

Small and large chopping knives: There's nothing more frustrating than a blunt knife. Keep them razor sharp with a good knife sharpener.

Bread knife

Grater: Four-sided with a choice of width options.

Vegetable peeler

Colander: Big enough to drain a pan of pasta!

Measuring jug: A multi-tasking type with measurements for both liquids and dry ingredients.

Mug: All mug measurements here are based on a 275ml/½ pint mug.

Set of spoon measurements

Flan case: Approx. 18cm/7 inch

Baking sheet

Wooden spoons and spatula

Potato masher

Rolling pin: Not essential but always useful.

Tea towels

Freezer-proof plastic tubs

Kitchen roll, foil and cling film

THE WISH LIST

Food processor: A joy to use and makes food prep so easy. If it's too much of a splurge, a stick blender makes a good compromise.

Toastie/griddle machine: The type fitted with griddle plates (rather than sandwich plates) is more versatile.

Slow cooker: Pop everything in the cooker and follow the maker's cooking times. Job done!

BELOW Buddha statues at a monastery near Inlay Lake, Burma

SHOPPING FOR THE BEST DEALS

Supermarkets have embraced the demand for world food ingredients and stock a wide selection of store-cupboard essentials for customers bitten by the travel bug. Having said that, although they are competitive on basics, unusual ingredients tend to be more expensive and sold in smaller quantities than in Asian or Middle Eastern shops.

These shops are great places to buy tinned tomatoes and pulses, bags of lentils, tahini, blocks of tofu, olives, spices, big bunches of herbs, exotic fruit and veg, and so on. They are always a mecca of fascinating ingredients. Street-market veg stalls are also a good source of bargain produce, particularly at the end of the day when boxes and bowls of fruit and veg are auctioned off. Buying in bulk offers the best deals. It's well worth getting a group together and sharing the cost.

There are ways and means to keep the bills down when shopping in a regular supermarket. Before hitting the aisles, run an eye over supermarket price-comparison sites on the internet to see who is offering the best deals. Buy fruit and veg loose. It's generally cheaper than prepackaged, and you can choose the exact quantity you need. Apply the same logic to shopping for meat and fish. Shop from the butcher and fish counter, unless there's an offer on prepackaged products that's too good to miss.

To avoid waste, freeze anything you can't use immediately or double up a recipe and freeze the results in portions. Frozen veg, fish and meat often cost less than fresh. They still retain all the goodness and you can defrost what you need a little at a time. Look out for end-of-the-day reductions, but be aware of the use-by date. It will probably be shorter than normal.

RIGHT Rialto market, Venice

VEGETARIAN STAPLES

Health food shops and supermarkets sell a wide selection of meat substitutes such as Quorn. Check the freezer section for the full range. Indian paneer cheese and Middle Eastern halloumi cheese are both excellent alternatives. They do not melt when cooked, so can be cubed or sliced and then fried or grilled until golden brown. Tofu is packed full of protein and comes plain, marinated, smoked or deep fried. If you are cooking with plain tofu, always buy the firm type, and remember tofu tends to be much cheaper in Oriental shops. For something different tempeh is another soy bean product, used in a similar way to tofu. You will find this in health food or Asian stores.

DECODING COOKING TERMS & USEFUL TIPS

Some terms are self-explanatory, but it's better to be safe than sorry.

Bring to the boil: Heat the pan over a high heat until bubbles and steam form. If a rapid boil is called for, keep the heat high.

Simmer: Simmering point is just below boiling point. To achieve a simmer once boiling point is reached, reduce the temperature until the bubbles in the pan have almost ceased but are still visible.

Heat the oil: It's important that cooking oil is hot before starting cooking. To test the oil is ready, place a small piece of the prepared ingredients in the pan. If it sizzles, the oil is ready.

Brown the meat: Browning meat gives a good flavour to a dish. Pat the meat dry with kitchen roll, heat the oil and quickly flash fry on both sides until the meat is brown on the outside but still only partially cooked inside.

Caramelize: The browning of naturally occurring sugars in food to give a caramel colour and a nutty flavour without burning. Cook slowly over a low heat and stir regularly.

Preheat the oven: An oven needs time to reach the correct temperature. Before starting cooking, arrange the oven shelves in position and turn the dial to the required temperature. Most ovens have a light that goes out when it's up to temperature. If there's no light, allow 15 minutes heating-up time.

Cooking with spices: To release the flavour from spices it's important they are cooked briefly in hot oil. Whole spices are generally added first, followed by ground spices that easily stick and burn unless kept constantly on the move. Store open packets of spices in separate, clean, screw-top jars.

Cooking with coconut milk: Never rapidly boil coconut milk. Overheating makes it 'split', resulting in a watery sauce.

Testing if cooked through: Always check meat and fish are properly cooked. Steak and lamb can be served pink in the middle. However, pork and chicken must be completely cooked through. To test, insert a sharp knife in the thickest part. If the juices run pink, the meat needs to be cooked for longer, until the juices run clear. To check fish, insert a fork: if it flakes easily the fish is ready.

Cooking pasta: Cooking times vary depending on type. Always read the cooking instructions on the packet first. Use a generous amount of water and make sure it's boiling rapidly before adding the pasta. Salt the water well and never cover the pan. The pasta is ready when it's *al dente* – soft but still retaining some bite.

How to cook rice: There's a knack to cooking rice and once you've cracked this you can't go wrong. To make two servings of white rice, half fill a mug with rice, tip it into a small pan and rinse in water three or four times – pouring off the excess water between rinses – until the water runs clear. Cover the washed rice with a mug of cold water and bring the pan to the boil. Reduce the heat to a minimum, cover the pan with a tight-fitting lid and continue to cook until all the water has been absorbed (approx. 10–15 minutes). Turn the heat off and leave the rice to sit in the covered pan for 10 minutes before fluffing with a fork. For brown rice, cover the same quantity of washed rice with a mug and a half of cold water and continue using the same method, allowing 20–25 minutes cooking time.

Rice tips: Fried rice is best made with cold pre-cooked rice. Store cooked rice in the fridge, always serve the fried rice piping hot and never reheat more than once or leave it out of the fridge.

Cans in fridge: Open cans in the fridge are a definite no-no. Transfer any remaining contents into a plastic tub.

Defrosting: Always place frozen fish, meat and pre-cooked food in the fridge to defrost. It takes longer but it's worth it to avoid bacteria multiplying. Serve food that has been frozen piping hot.

Stock: There are many different types of stock on the market. Fresh (from the chiller compartment) is more like homemade but comes at a higher price. Alternatively, look for stock cubes or powder with natural ingredients and no added MSG.

Have all the ingredients prepared and ready to go before starting to cook.

EUROPA
Politische Übersicht.

Maßstab 1:25 000 000.

Deutsche Meilen (15=1°)

Kilometer 111,3=1°

Die Hauptstädte sind unterstrichen.

EUROPE: INTERRAIL CULTURE VULTURES

A trip to Europe still offers fantastic value for money if you are canny with your cash. Ride the tracks for a whirlwind mystery tour of the cultural and gastronomic highs of Europe, the modern equivalent of the Grand Tour. Revel in history, architecture, art and music. Discover hidden haunts and out of the way cafés and absorb the many different cultures en route.

To cut the cost of hotel bills, crash out on overnight trains between locations, saving valuable euros to sample the countless cuisines on the way. Stock up on provisions at local markets and delectable delis for al fresco feasts. And when in cafés and bars on the Continent, follow the lead of the regulars. Stand at the bar or take a seat inside to avoid the higher rates for the same food and drink at outside tables. It's a guaranteed way to gather valuable insiders' tips on what's happening, and soak up the local atmosphere.

Snack at patisseries and prix fixe cafés in the boulevards of Paris, munch frites and mayo in Amsterdam and sober up with a schnitzel sandwich at Munich's beer-fuelled Oktoberfest. Shun pricey restaurants on the grand squares of Italy in favour of side-street trattorias serving steaming bowls of homemade pasta or pizza oozing with toppings. Take tapas in a bar in Barcelona or raciones in the Boqueria market, and when island hopping in the Aegean sunbathe on the terrace of a beachside taverna with a meze lunch, a glass of ouzo and a view of the brilliant blue sea.

CLOCKWISE FROM LEFT Beach at
Pescoluse, Puglia; Boqueria market
in Barcelona; a trattoria in Venice;
Saturday market in St Tropez;
Piazza San Marco in Venice

THE EUROPEAN STORE CUPBOARD

Stock up on pasta, tinned tomatoes and dairy products, with the addition of dried and fresh herbs, and a couple of spices to add Mediterranean flavour.

Dairy: Natural yoghurt and cream. Cheese-wise: Parmesan, mozzarella, Cheddar and feta.

Eggs: Free range if you can afford them.

Tomatoes: Tinned chopped tomatoes and tomato purée for the cupboard and fresh for the fridge. Choose ripe red varieties for the best flavour.

Pasta: Spaghetti and tagliatelle are the most useful. The recipes will work with most types of pasta if you already have a packet open.

Ready-made pastry: Buy ready-rolled in a packet.

Olive oil: It's more expensive than vegetable oil but it does make a difference. To keep the shopping bill down, avoid the top-end extra virgin oils.

Olives: Middle Eastern supermarkets sell value packs of olives in all shapes and sizes.

Herbs: Dried thyme and oregano. Buy small packs as they lose their flavour over time. Grow pots of fresh mint, basil and parsley (available from supermarkets) on a sunny window ledge for a constant supply of fresh herbs.

Spices: Ground cumin and paprika. To give Spanish recipes an authentic taste it's worth investing in pimentón (smoked ground paprika). It comes in two types — sweet or spicy. Choose whichever you prefer.

Lemon juice: Stick to fresh every time.

RIGHT Olive grove in Salento

QUICHE LORRAINE

MAKES 4 SLICES

Homemade quiche tastes infinitely better than shop-bought. Using ready-rolled pastry makes a good short cut. Serve warm from the oven.

YOU NEED

- 1 pack chilled ready-rolled pastry
- 110g/4oz smoked streaky bacon
- Vegetable oil to fry
- 3 large eggs
- 275ml/½ pint double cream
- 75g/3oz grated Cheddar cheese
- Salt and black pepper
- 18cm/7 inch flan case (or loose-bottomed flan tin)

HOW

- Preheat the oven to 190°C/375°F/gas mark 5.
- Grease the flan case with butter. Be generous with the butter — it makes taking out the cut pieces of quiche much easier.
- Unroll the pastry and line the flan case, gently pressing the pastry into the corners leaving a 1cm/½ inch overlap.
- Fold the excess pastry over the edge of the tin — this prevents the pastry shrinking — and prick the bottom with a fork.

STREET STALL AUTHENTIC

Use grated Gruyère cheese instead of Cheddar.

VEGETARIAN?
Replace bacon bits with a handful of fried sliced mushrooms or parboiled broccoli florets.

LIGHTER OPTION?
Use half the quantity of cream and make up the difference with milk.

FREEZE any leftover pastry.

- Line the pastry case with tin foil scrunched around the edges to keep it in place.
- Place on the middle shelf of the preheated oven and cook for 10 minutes, then remove the foil and cook for a further 10 minutes. (If the pastry rises, don't worry. It will sink down again as it cools.)
- While the pastry is cooking, slice the bacon into strips and fry in a splash of oil until golden brown. Whisk the eggs and cream together with a fork until light and frothy. Stir in half the cheese and season with salt and black pepper to taste.
- Pour the egg mixture into the pastry case and sprinkle the bacon bits and the rest of the cheese evenly on top.
- Carefully place the quiche back in the oven and bake for a further 30 minutes until the top is golden and the middle set. Remove from the oven and leave to sit for a further 10 minutes before cutting away the excess pastry overlap with a sharp knife.

CAFÉ SOCIETY IN PARIS

So much to see! Wonderful museums, regal tree-lined avenues, ornamental gardens, flea markets, and famous monuments that still retain their magic even though we have seen them a million times before in pictures. Sunbathe on the summer beaches along the Seine, discover whether you prefer the Left Bank or the Right Bank and be bamboozled by fantastical street performers. All this pavement battering builds up an appetite. Snack on thick slices of warm quiche, picnic on baguettes filled with 'fromage' or slurp a bowl of onion soup topped with a fat cheesy crouton.

FRENCH ONION SOUP

MAKES 4 SERVINGS

The secret to making an authentic French onion soup is to cook the onions slowly over a low heat until they become soft and caramelized. The cheesy crouton is traditionally topped with Gruyère but any cheaper cheese that melts well can be used instead.

YOU NEED

- 2 tablespoons butter
- 2 tablespoons vegetable oil
- 700g/1½ lb onions, thinly sliced
- 2 garlic cloves, finely chopped
- ½ teaspoon sugar

- 1.2 litres/2 pints beef or vegetable stock
- ½ teaspoon dried thyme
- Salt and black pepper

THE CHEESY CROUTONS
- Diagonally cut thick slices of baguette
- Grated cheese

STREET STALL AUTHENTIC

Add a splash of red wine to the caramelized onions, cook for a few minutes until reduced, then pour in the stock.

HOW

- Heat the butter and oil in a saucepan. When the butter starts to foam, add the onions and garlic and cook, stirring regularly, until the onions become soft but not brown.
- Stir in the sugar, reduce the heat to a minimum, cover the pan and continue to cook, stirring every once in a while, until the onions become golden and caramelized.
- Add the stock and thyme, season with salt and black pepper to taste and gently simmer for 15 minutes.
- To make the croutons, toast the baguette slices until crunchy and golden, and generously coat with grated cheese. Place under a hot grill and cook until the cheese is molten and starting to brown.

COOKING TIP
Don't rush cooking the onions or they'll burn.

SERVE
Ladle the soup into deep bowls and float the cheesy croutons on top.

FRITES IN AMSTERDAM

Be bold and experimental, indulge the alternative in the canal cafés of Amsterdam. Anything goes in the lively arty scene: poetry and pornography, theatre and acrobatics, thrift shops and funky boutiques. Rent a bike and peddle along canal-side paths past a higgledy-piggledy mishmash of architectural marvels and curved bridges. Read up on Rembrandt and Van Gogh. Keep the energy levels up with the fast-food favourite — frites and peanut sauce.

Along the canals of Amsterdam

PEANUT SAUCE

MAKES A SMALL BOWL

Dollop on to fries, or take the healthy route and use as a protein-rich dip for raw vegetable crudités, or a short-cut satay-style sauce to accompany grilled meat or fish. Take your pick!

YOU NEED
- 3 tablespoons smooth peanut butter
- 2 teaspoons lemon juice
- I teaspoon runny honey
- 120ml/4fl oz mayonnaise
- ½ teaspoon ground cayenne pepper or chilli (or to taste)
- ½ teaspoon paprika
- Salt

HOW
- Mix the peanut butter with the lemon juice and honey, then stir in the mayonnaise, ground cayenne, paprika and salt to taste.

STREET STALL AUTHENTIC

Serve with homemade frites: peel waxy potatoes and cut into thin chips, then shallow fry in vegetable oil until golden brown on the outside and soft in the middle.

COOKING TIP
Cut a selection of vegetable sticks such as celery, cucumber, pepper and carrot.

OKTOBERFEST MUNCHIES IN MUNICH

Don the lederhosen or dirndl skirt and raise a 'Mass' of München beer at the largest people festival in the world. It's all the fun of the fair with parades and side-stalls, beer, dare-devil rides, beer, revelry, beer . . . and more beer!

SERVE

With potato salad: coat diced boiled potatoes with equal quantities of seasoned mayonnaise and natural yoghurt (as much or as little as you like), then sprinkle with sliced spring onions.

FESTIVAL SCHNITZEL

MAKES 2

Prepare for the party with a pork schnitzel — you can use turkey or chicken fillets if you prefer, the only must being that the meat is pounded until thin. Make your own breadcrumbs by grating any leftover dry bread or pick up a pack in a supermarket or good bakery. Serve with potato salad and watercress, or sandwich style inside a bun with sliced tomato, lettuce and a squirt of mayo.

YOU NEED

- 2 boneless pork loin chops
- ½ mug dry breadcrumbs
- Grated zest of ½ lemon
- 2 tablespoons plain flour
- 1 medium egg, beaten
- Salt and black pepper
- 2 dessertspoons butter
- 1 tablespoon vegetable oil

HOW

- Trim the fat from the chops and pop each one into a separate plastic bag. Place on a chopping board and bash with a rolling pin or the side of a tin — chickpeas, tomatoes, whatever's in the cupboard — until each chop is about 5mm/¼ inch thick.
- Mix the breadcrumbs and lemon zest together in a shallow bowl and place the flour and the beaten egg in two separate shallow bowls.
- Season the pork with salt and black pepper to taste and dip first in the flour, then the egg and finally the breadcrumbs until well coated on each side.
- Heat the butter and oil in a frying pan. When the butter starts to foam, fry the chops over a medium heat for 3–4 minutes on each side until the breadcrumbs are golden brown and crisp and the pork is cooked through.

STREET STALL AUTHENTIC

Squeeze a wedge of lemon over the schnitzel.

THE GONDOLIERS' CAFÉS OF VENICE

Leave the crowds behind and delve into the eerie backstreets of this unique and romantic floating city. Hear the echo of your footsteps and the clatter of daily life from open windows as you navigate the crumbling canal-side walkways. Expect to get lost. It's obligatory. You'll be well rewarded with hidden historic surprises, quiet squares and secret trattorias, before stumbling back on track to the buzz of San Marco or the Rialto Bridge.

Gondoliers in Venice

SPAGHETTI CARBONARA

SERVES 2

Fast food the Italian way.

YOU NEED

- 225g/8oz spaghetti (or tagliatelle)
- 150g/5oz streaky bacon, cut into strips
- 1 tablespoon olive or vegetable oil
- 2 large eggs, beaten
- 5 tablespoons double cream
- 50g/2oz grated Parmesan cheese
- Salt and plenty of black pepper

HOW

- Two-thirds fill a medium-size pan with water. Add half a teaspoon of salt and bring the water to the boil.
- Lower the pasta into the boiling water and as it starts to soften encourage it to immerse properly with a wooden spoon, separating any clumps that form. Cook the pasta as instructed on the packet until just soft.
- While the pasta is cooking, fry the bacon strips in the olive oil until golden brown and crunchy.
- Beat the eggs and cream together until light and fluffy. Stir in three quarters of the Parmesan and season with salt to taste.
- When the pasta is ready, scoop half a mug of pasta water from the pan, then drain the pasta. Return the pasta to the pan.
- Pour in the egg mixture and two tablespoons of the pasta water and stir immediately and continuously (to prevent the egg scrambling) until a creamy, glossy sauce evenly coats the pasta. Add extra water if necessary to maintain a thick sauce.
- Add the bacon bits, season with plenty of black pepper and sprinkle with the remaining grated Parmesan on top.

STREET STALL AUTHENTIC

Cook a couple of crushed garlic cloves with the bacon.

VEGETARIAN?
Swap the bacon for thinly sliced mushrooms.

LEFT The Amalfi coast

AUBERGINE PARMIGIANA

SERVES 2

Serve this veggie bake with salad and chunks of focaccia bread.

YOU NEED

- An ovenproof dish
  (approx. 20cm/8 inches in diameter)
- I large aubergine, cut into 0.5cm/
  ¼ inch slices
- Olive oil
- I small onion, diced
- I clove garlic, finely chopped
- 400g/14oz tin chopped tomatoes
- 2 tablespoon tomato purée
- I teaspoon sugar or honey
- A small handful of basil leaves,
  roughly chopped
- 25g/1oz grated Parmesan cheese
  (about 6 tablespoons)
- I ball of mozzarella, sliced and broken
  into chunks
- Salt and black pepper

STREET STALL AUTHENTIC

Add Half a teaspoon of dried oregano to the tomato sauce.

SHORT OF TIME?

Use ready-made tomato and basil sauce.

HOW

- Rub the aubergine slices on both sides with a little olive oil and season with a light sprinkling of salt.
- Heat a frying pan and cook the aubergine slices on both sides until charred and soft. (There's no need to add extra oil.)
- To make the sauce, heat a couple of tablespoons of olive oil in a small saucepan and fry the onion and garlic until soft. Stir in the chopped tomatoes, tomato purée and sugar. Season to taste, cover the pan and gently simmer for 10 minutes before adding the basil.
- Preheat the oven to 200°C/400°F/ gas mark 6.
- To assemble the aubergine bake, coat the bottom of the ovenproof dish with half the tomato sauce, cover with half the aubergine (in an overlapping layer) and sprinkle with half the Parmesan and mozzarella cheese. Layer the remaining ingredients in the same order, ending with the cheese.
- Place the dish in the preheated oven and cook for 30–35 minutes until the bake is bubbling hot and the cheese is golden brown.

TAPAS ON A SPANISH SQUARE

Sample a colourful snapshot of day-to-day Spanish life in the hub of the neighbourhood, a local bar in the central square. It offers excellent entertainment value from early morning breakfast to raucous late-night supper. Small dishes of bite-size tapas are served throughout the day. Chattering friends catch up over a plate or two with a cerveza or a copa di vino while the kids practise their flamenco moves in the square. Tapas can be as simple as a plate of cheese and olives or as complex as sizzling stuffed squid or eggs topped with pepper and tomato sauce and spicy sausage. Ask for a larger ración if you're particularly tempted.

Trujillo Extremadura

CHICKPEAS, SPINACH & MUSHROOMS ON TOAST

SERVES 2

This tapa staple couldn't be simpler. Pile on to garlicky toast for a stress-free supper on the sofa.

YOU NEED

- 2 tablespoons olive oil
- 1 small onion, diced
- 1 garlic clove, crushed
- ½ teaspoon ground cumin
- ½ teaspoon ground paprika (or pimentón)
- 175g/6oz spinach, washed and roughly chopped (or frozen chopped spinach)
- ½ mug tinned chickpeas
- ⅓ mug chickpea water from the tin
- 75g/3oz oyster or chestnut mushrooms, thickly sliced
- A squeeze of lemon juice
- Salt and black pepper
- Thick slices of crusty bread
- 1 garlic clove
- Olive oil

HOW

- Heat the olive oil in a frying pan, add the onion and garlic and cook until soft.
- Stir in the spices and cook for a few seconds before adding the spinach.
- As the spinach starts to wilt, add the chickpeas, chickpea water and the sliced mushrooms.
- Lightly crush the chickpeas with the back of a wooden spoon and continue to cook for a few minutes until the liquid reduces and the mushrooms are just cooked.
- Add a good squeeze of lemon juice and season with salt and pepper to taste.
- Toast the bread, rub one side with the garlic clove and drizzle with olive oil. Spoon the spinach and chickpea mixture on top.

STREET STALL AUTHENTIC

Top with wafer-thin slices of Manchego cheese.

COOKING TIP

Cook strips of bacon with the onions for a more filling meal.

PIPERRADA SCRAMBLED EGGS

SERVES 2

Piperrada pepper and tomato sauce is
a top accompaniment to eggs in Spain.
For perfect scrambled eggs, remove the
pan from the heat before the egg looks
completely cooked — the egg continues to
cook until served.

YOU NEED

- 2 tablespoons olive oil
- I medium onion, diced
- ½ green pepper, diced
- ½ red pepper, diced
- I garlic clove, crushed
- I teaspoon pimentón (or ground
  paprika)
- ½ a 400g/14oz tin chopped tomatoes
- 4 large eggs
- I teaspoon chopped parsley (optional)
- Salt and black pepper

STREET STALL AUTHENTIC

Serve with bread, a dish of olives and thick slices of spicy chorizo sausage (skin removed) fried in olive oil until crunchy.

HOW

- Heat the olive oil in a frying pan. Add the onion, peppers and garlic and fry until soft.
- Stir in the pimentón, cook for a couple of seconds, then add the chopped tomatoes.
- Season with salt and pepper to taste and simmer for 10 minutes or so until the sauce thickens.
- To make the scrambled eggs, beat the egg with the chopped parsley and season to taste.
- Heat a non-stick frying pan, add a large knob of butter and swirl it around the bottom of the pan until melted.
- Pour in the eggs, and stir constantly with a wooden spoon until the egg has a slightly runny scrambled-egg texture. Remove immediately from the heat, spoon on to plates and serve topped with spoonfuls of the hot piperrada sauce.

COOKING TIP

Try the sauce with an omelette or grilled meat.

A GREEK MEZE OVERLOOKING THE AEGEAN SEA

Round off the Interrail experience with a spot of sun and sea worship Greek Island hopping in the Med. Dive into crystal-clear waters from tranquil shores, explore the ghostly remnants of tumbling archeological sites, and walk to white-washed villages along donkey-worn mountainous paths, fragrant with the scent of wild herbs. Graze meze-style on burningly hot courgette fritters cooled with yoghurty tatziki, lemony grilled meat and fish, plump olives, warm pitta bread and, of course, Greek salad.

A deserted beach in the Ionian Islands

COURGETTE & FETA FRITTERS

MAKES 8

Simply dip these courgette fritters into tatziki or stuff inside toasted pitta bread with mixed salad leaves, tomato and a drizzle of the yoghurty sauce.

YOU NEED

- 1 medium courgette (about 175g/6oz), coarsely grated
- 1 small egg, beaten
- 2 heaped tablespoons plain flour
- ¼ medium onion, finely chopped
- 50g/2oz crumbled feta cheese
- 1 tablespoon chopped mint leaves (or parsley)
- Salt and black pepper
- Oil to fry (preferably olive)

For the tzatziki dip
- 1 small pot Greek-style yoghurt
- 2 tablespoons olive oil
- 1 tablespoon lemon juice
- 6 cm/2½ inch chunk of cucumber, coarsely grated
- 1 garlic clove, crushed
- 1 teaspoon chopped dill (or mint)
- Salt and black pepper

STREET STALL AUTHENTIC

Serve with pickled green chillies (sold in jars).

COOKING TIP

Squeeze as much water as you can from the grated courgette. Use the batter straight away.

HOW

- Place the grated courgette in a clean tea towel or in a sieve and squeeze away as much water as possible.
- Mix the beaten egg with the flour until well combined.
- Stir in the courgette, onion, feta and mint and season with salt and pepper to taste.
- Heat a couple of tablespoons of oil in a non-stick frying pan and scoop tablespoons of the mixture into the pan.
- Gently flatten the fritters with a spatula and fry for a few minutes on each side until golden brown and crunchy.
- To make the tzatziki, lightly whip the yoghurt, olive oil and lemon juice together with a fork, then stir in the cucumber, garlic and dill and season to taste.

Greece

GREEK SALAD

SERVES 2

A rustic feta cheese salad made with the vegetables grown in a typical Greek garden.

YOU NEED

- 4 ripe tomatoes, cut in chunks
- ⅓ medium cucumber, cut in chunks
- ½ small green pepper, thinly sliced
- A scattering of thinly sliced red onion
- 1 small Little Gem lettuce, thickly sliced
- 125g/4½oz block of feta cheese, cut in half
- A small handful of black olives
- Toasted pitta bread to serve

DRESSING

- 2 tablespoons olive oil
- 1 dessertspoon lemon juice
- ¼ teaspoon dried oregano (plus a little extra)
- Salt and black pepper to taste

HOW

- Place the dressing ingredients in a mug and whisk together with a fork.
- Mix the chopped tomatoes, cucumber, pepper and red onion in a bowl. Add the dressing and gently toss together until the vegetables are well coated.
- Divide the lettuce between two plates and pile the salad on top, dot with olives and top with the feta cheese.
- Sprinkle the feta with a little extra oregano.

STREET STALL AUTHENTIC

Mix a tablespoon of capers with the salad.

COOKING TIP

Serve with grilled pork chops or fried fish drizzled with a dash of olive oil, a squeeze of lemon juice and a sprinkling of dried oregano.

CARIBBEAN SEA

Honduras
Nicaragua
Costa Rica
S. Juan
Limon
Colo.
S. José
Cocos I.
G. of Panama
Panama
Galapagos

VENEZUELA
Caracas
Bolivar
Medellin
Bogotá
COLOMBIA
Popayan
Pasto
Quito
Chimborazo 20,520
ECUADOR
Guayaquil
Pto. Parina
Payta
Lobos I.
Lambayeque
Trujillo
Chimbote
Callao

P E R U
Loreto
Teffe
Tabatinga
R. Napo
R. Javary
R. Huallaga
Marañon

Orinoco
R. Parima
Cassiquiare
Isabel
Rio Negro
Manáos
R. Yapura
R. Putumayo

Caraccas
P. Cabello
La Guaira
Guayana
Brit.
Dutch
R. Essequibo
George town
R. Coventyne
R. Surinam
R. Maroni
R. Oyapock
Maraça I.
R. Amazon
Marajo I.
Rio Pará
Obidos
Santarem
Para
Viana
Maranhão
Parnahyba
Ceara
Therezina
Oeiras
Natal
Pernambuco
Maceio
Alagoas
R. São Francisco

St. Lucia (Br.)
Barbados (Br.)
Tobago (Br.)
Trinidad (Br.)

Fernando
Noronha
C. San Roque

BRAZIL
Cuyaba
Goyaz
Sta. Cruz
P. Imperial
Barral
Bahia
Todos os Santos
Belmonte
Porto Seguro
Minas Geraes
Diamantina
Ouro Preto
Rio Doce
Victoria
R. Parahyba
Campos
Rio de Janeiro

B O L I V I A
La Paz
Sucre
S. Cruz
R. Mamore
R. Beni
R. Guapore
Corumba
Concepcion
Tacna
Arica
Tarapaca
Iquique
Cobija
Mejillones
Antofagasta
Taltal
S. Ambrosio
S. Felix
Caldera
Copiapo
Potosi
Tarija

PARAGUAY
Asuncion
Corrientes
Uruguayana

C H I L E
A R G E N T I N A
Tucuman
Rioja
Cordova
Mendoza
Rosario
Salta
S. Fé
Aconcagua 22,860
Juan Fernandez
Mas-a-Fuera
Valparaiso
Santiago
Talca
Talcahuana
Concepcion
Valdivia
Puerto Montt
Ancud
Chiloe
Chonos Arch.
Taytao Pen.
Wellington I.
Atacama

URU-
GUAY
Fray Bentos
Montevideo
Rio de la Plata
C. San Antonio
Mar del Plata
C. Corrientes
Buenos Aires
La Plata
Porto Alegre
Lagoa dos Patos
Rio Grande do Sul
Curitiba
Cananea
Paranagua
S. Francisco
Sta. Catharina I.
Testerro
S. Paulo
Santos

P A T A G O N I A
R. Colorado
R. Negro
Bahia Blanca
Carmen de Patagones
G. of S. Matias
Rawson
Chubut
G. of St George
P. Desire
Santa Cruz
Magellan's Str.
C. Pillar
C. Virgins
Tierra del Fuego
Staten I.
Falkland I. (Brit.)
Stanley
South Georgia (Brit.)

PACIFIC OCEAN
ATLANTIC OCEAN
SOUTH
Tropic of Capricorn

SOUTH AMERICA: ON THE INCA TRAIL

The diverse terrain of the Andes, which run like a gigantic craggy spine along the length of South America, has shaped the diet of the local population. The Incas harnessed the harshness of the terrain, building intricate agricultural terraces to maximize crop growth at all altitudes. Particularly partial to their indigenous potatoes, they cultivated hundreds of multi-coloured varieties, all with different tastes and textures. Potatoes are still king of South American cuisine, and appear in almost every dish in some shape or form. Tomatoes, peppers, chilli, corn and beans are also native to the Andes, and the benefits of quinoa have been known here for centuries.

Meat-wise — vegetarians cover your eyes — guinea pigs, llamas and alpacas are viewed in a favourable light in parts of South America, providing a carnivorous staple. Luckily for them, Spanish conquistadors imported cattle, pigs and sheep along with their cooking styles.

They also brought crates of wine, and the know-how to cultivate and produce it locally. Sample the fruits of their labour in the haciendas, comedors and bars along the way. More recently, Chinese and Japanese settlers have created an interesting combination of Asian and local cuisine, and Italians have shared their love of pasta and pizza, a lifesaver for westerners craving something more familiar.

Pastry empanadas bulging with sweet and savoury fillings and corn humitas (or tamales depending on which country you're in) offer a welcome grab-and-go snack, excellent washed down with fluorescent yellow Inca Cola. These are rarely meat free, so eating here often isn't easy for vegetarians. Pescatarians won't find it quite as difficult, the massive coastline providing a constant supply of all things fishy. Put aside any preconceptions and try ceviche, raw fish cured in citrus juice topped with chilli and onion. Avoid street stalls on this one occasion. Ceviche must be really fresh or you won't be trying it a second time!

CLOCKWISE FROM BELOW
Crossing the Andes by the Travesía route in Chile; an Inca Trail bus; a street food stall in Cuba; the Calchaquies valley in Argentina; Cachi, Argentina.

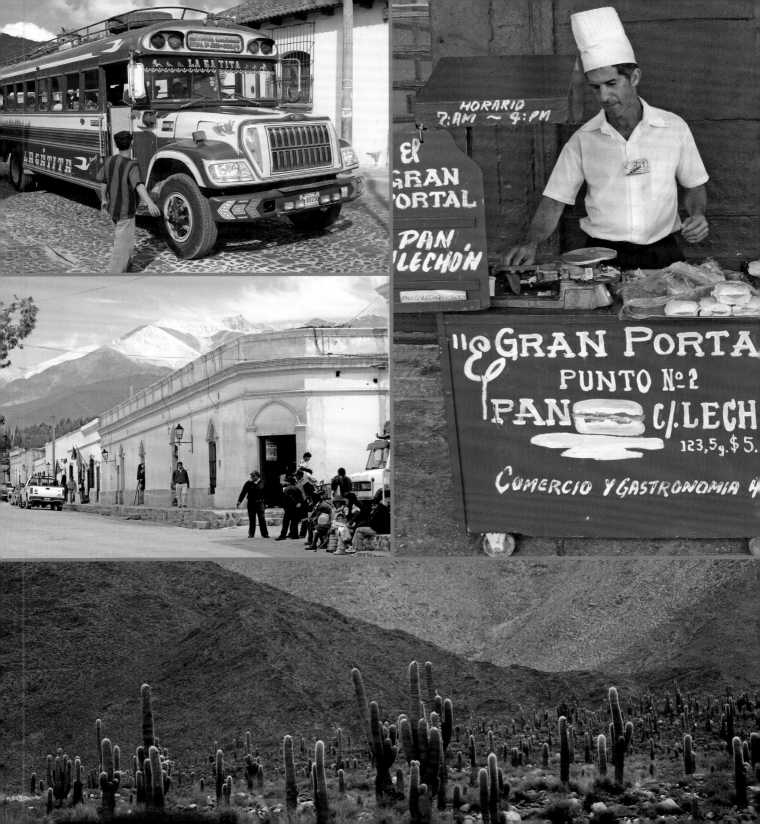

THE SOUTH AMERICAN STORE CUPBOARD

The conquistadors added Spanish flavours to the South American store cupboard. These are combined with homegrown staples such as potatoes, peppers, chillies and green beans. Stock up on other classic South American ingredients — tinned (or frozen) sweetcorn, pulses and chopped tomatoes — and you can't go wrong.

Ground paprika: Preferably the smoked variety (pimentón).

Ground cumin

Quinoa: The Andean high-protein grain, used in a similar way to rice.

Rice: Spanish paella rice or short-grain white rice.

Dried oregano

Red wine vinegar: Lemon juice or red wine can be used instead.

Chorizo: Smoky-flavoured salami-style sausage.

Olives and olive oil

Peanut butter: Preferably smooth.

Hot sauce: Tabasco is always handy.

Fresh coriander and parsley

HANGING OUT IN THE HACIENDAS OF CUZCO

Catch your breath in the cobbled streets of Cuzco, among the ruins of the legendary Inca capital. Acclimatize to the dizzying altitude with copious cups of coca tea in a laid-back plaza café and immerse yourself in the grisly history of pre-Columbian Peru. Recharged, trek past grazing llamas and dramatic mountains to sleepy villages that burst into life on market day. Bargain for crazy, colourful ponchos from mad-hatted locals, hang out at haciendas with ceviche and a pisco sour or, for those with a strong stomach and a taste for the authentic, a glass of corn beer and some fried guinea pig.

All paths lead to Machu Picchu. Climb to the summit of Huayna Picchu and perch among the clouds at the temple of the Inca high priest as the sun rises over the iconic lost city. In this, the original home of the potato and the chilli, the starchy staple and its fiery friend are combined to make stews, rice dishes and Peruvian-style stir-fries to fuel a day trekking and chilly evenings.

Vicuna, Chile

COOKING TIP

Buy ready-diced chicken. It tends to be cheaper.

VEGETARIAN?

Use Quorn meat-free 'chicken' fillets, or stick to veg and add a handful of diced butternut squash at the same time as the onion and red pepper.

ARROZ CON POLLO

SERVES 2

Rice and chicken hits the spot after a long day hiking on the Inca Trail.

YOU NEED

- 2 tablespoons olive oil
- I medium onion, finely chopped
- ½ red pepper, diced
- I garlic clove, finely chopped
- I red chilli, finely chopped (optional)
- 250g/9oz chicken, diced
- ½ teaspoon ground cumin and paprika
- I tablespoon tomato purée
- A small bunch of coriander, finely chopped
- ½ mug paella or short-grain rice
- I mug chicken or vegetable stock
- ½ mug frozen peas and sweetcorn mixed together
- Salt and black pepper

HOW

- Heat the olive oil in a saucepan (with a lid) and fry the onion, pepper, garlic and chilli until just soft.
- Add the chicken and continue to cook until the meat is brown on all sides.
- Stir in the spices and rice until everything is evenly coated with spice.
- Add the tomato purée and coriander and pour in the stock.
- Add the peas and sweetcorn, and season with salt and pepper to taste.
- Bring the pan to a simmer, cover with a lid and continue to cook until the stock is completely absorbed and the chicken is cooked through.
- Leave the rice to stand in the covered pan for 5 minutes, then fluff with a fork before serving.

STREET STALL AUTHENTIC

Use beer in place of stock.
Serve with tomato salsa: mix a couple of diced tomatoes with a small handful of finely chopped red onion, a tablespoon of chopped parsley and a good squeeze of lemon juice.

LEFT Machu Picchu

LOMO SALTADO: PERUVIAN BEEF STIR-FRY

SERVES 2

A typical example of Chinese cooking with a Peruvian twist dished up in canteen-style cafés known locally as 'chiffas'. Potatoes even make their way into stir-fries, and it's quite normal for a pile of rice to be served on the side — passable if you're walking all day. To avoid packing on the pounds back home, stick to one or the other. When the bank balance is low, replace steak with diagonally sliced frankfurters or sausages.

YOU NEED

- 2 medium potatoes, peeled, cut in half lengthwise and thinly sliced
- Vegetable oil to fry
- I smallish red onion, thinly sliced
- 2 garlic cloves, finely chopped
- 2 medium frying steaks, seasoned with salt and cut into Icm/½ inch strips
- 2 medium tomatoes, cut in half, seeds scooped out and sliced thickly
- I red chilli, thinly sliced lengthwise
- I tablespoon dark soy sauce
- I dessertspoon red wine vinegar
- A small handful of parsley leaves, finely chopped
- Salt and black pepper

STREET STALL AUTHENTIC

Add a generous tablespoon of pisco, tequila or beer at the same time as the soy sauce.
Smother with hot Tabasco sauce.

COOKING TIP

Use frying steak. It's good value and cooks quickly. Avoid overcooking or it will become tough.

VEGETARIAN?

Use Quorn meat-free 'steak' strips or sliced vegetarian sausages

HOW

- To make the sautéed potatoes, coat the bottom of a frying pan with vegetable oil, heat the oil, place the sliced potatoes in a single layer and cook until golden brown on both sides and soft in the middle. Place the potatoes in a bowl and cover with a plate to keep warm.

- If the frying pan looks dry, add an extra tablespoon of oil before adding the onion and garlic and cooking until soft.

- Add the beef and briefly stir-fry until the meat is browned on all sides.

- Add the tomatoes and chilli and stir-fry for a minute or so before adding the soy sauce, vinegar and parsley.

- Season with black pepper and salt to taste and stir-fry for a few seconds longer until the liquid ingredients have reduced.

- Pile the stir-fry on plates and top with the sautéed potatoes.

SOPA DE MANI

MAKES 4 GENEROUS PORTIONS

If you're feeling ravenous, serve this Andean peanut and potato soup with the best bits of plato paceño — boiled sweetcorn cobs smothered in butter and thick slices of halloumi or mozzarella cheese fried in olive oil until golden.

YOU NEED

- 2 tablespoons vegetable oil
- 1 medium onion, finely chopped
- 2 garlic cloves, finely chopped
- 2 medium baking potatoes (approx. 560g/1¼lb), peeled and diced
- 1 teaspoon ground cumin
- 1 teaspoon dried oregano
- 600ml/1 pint vegetable stock
- 1 medium carrot, finely diced
- ½ red or green pepper, diced
- A handful of green beans, cut into pea-size rounds
- 200ml/7fl oz milk
- 4 tablespoons smooth peanut butter, thinned with a splash of hot water
- 1 heaped tablespoon finely chopped parsley or coriander leaves
- Salt and black pepper

STREET STALL AUTHENTIC

Dollop with spicy llajhua sauce. To make the sauce, blend or mash a third of a tin of chopped tomatoes with a tablespoon of olive oil, a shake of salt, and finely chopped onion, chilli and coriander leaves to taste.

COOKING TIP

Make a big pan of soup and share with friends or freeze in portions.

HOW

- Heat the oil in a saucepan, add the onion and garlic and cook until soft but not brown.
- Add the potatoes and continue to cook until the potatoes start to soften.
- Stir in the cumin and oregano, cook for a couple of seconds, then pour in the stock.
- Cover the pan and simmer the soup until the potatoes are soft and starting to break down.
- Lightly crush the potatoes with a potato masher or fork, then stir in the carrot, pepper, beans, milk and thinned peanut butter.
- Season with salt and black pepper to taste and continue to simmer, stirring regularly, until the vegetables are cooked.
- Ladle the soup into deep bowls and sprinkle with chopped parsley (or coriander).

LONG LUNCHES IN THE COMEDORS OF BOLIVIA

Bolivia breaks world records. La Paz, clinging to the valleys of soaring snow-capped mountains, clocks in as the world's highest capital, pipped at the post as the world's highest city by Bolivia's colonial-era Potosi. Glassy Lake Titicaca, with its astonishing inhabited floating reed islands scores first place in the highest navigable lakes stakes, and the dazzling white lunar landscape of the Salar de Uyuni is officially the flattest place on earth. Ride like the wind on the dare-devil mountain bike ride down the Yungas Road and you will have survived the most dangerous road in the world.

Everything stops for a long leisurely lunch in Bolivia. A hearty bowl of soup is invariably followed by the vegetarian speciality plato paceño — sweetcorn cobs served with fried cheese and potatoes — or meat lovers can munch through the mound of fried steak and sausage in the famous Bolivian pique a lo macho plate.

QUINOA & BEAN STEW

SERVES 2

A protein-packed, wholesome supper. Top with crumbled feta or any grated cheese.

YOU NEED

- ½ mug quinoa
- 2 tablespoons olive (or vegetable) oil
- 1 smallish onion, diced
- 1 garlic clove, finely chopped
- 1 celery stalk, diced
- ½ red pepper, diced
- A handful of diced sweet potato (or regular potato)
- 1 teaspoon paprika
- ½ teaspoon ground cumin
- Chilli powder to taste
- ⅓ mug tinned or frozen sweetcorn
- ½ a 400g/14oz tin butter beans, chickpeas or kidney beans
- ½ a 400g/14oz tin chopped tomatoes
- ⅓ mug water
- A small handful of chopped parsley
- Salt and black pepper

SMALL BUDGET?

Replace the quinoa with cooked brown rice if quinoa is beyond your budget.

STREET STALL AUTHENTIC

Add a small handful of roughly chopped pitted olives at the same time as the chopped parsley.

HOW

- Place the quinoa in a small saucepan and cover with a mug of cold water. Bring the pan to a simmer, cover with a lid and continue to cook until all the water has been absorbed – this should take 10–15 minutes. Leave the quinoa to sit in the covered pan for 10 minutes before fluffing with a fork.
- Heat the oil in a separate saucepan and fry the onion and garlic until soft but not brown.
- Add the celery, pepper and sweet potato and continue to cook until just soft.
- Add the paprika, cumin and chilli and cook, stirring constantly, until the vegetables are coated in spices.
- Stir in the sweetcorn, beans, tomato and water.
- Cover the pan and gently simmer until the vegetables are soft.
- Add the chopped parsley, season with salt and pepper to taste and simmer for a further 5 minutes.
- Place the quinoa in the bottom of a bowl, spoon the stew over the top and sprinkle with cheese.

THE MENU DEL DIA IN THE ATACAMA

Lose yourself in the Dali-esque landscapes of the Atacama Desert. It has to be seen to be believed. Steaming geysers, bubbling mud, eerie salt flats where the wind whistles, pink flamingos paddling in shimmering lagoons, vertiginous volcanoes and the unforgettable sight of sunset's golden glow illuminating sculpted dunes and stone formations etched by the elements. Picnic on completo hot dogs, piled high with toppings, and wedges of eggy tortilla.

Back in the tiny oasis town of San Pedro de Atacama, cruise the dusty backstreets lined with sun-baked clay houses to find a local comedor and take a punt on the set menu of the day that can't be beaten for value, even with a glass of homegrown Chilean wine.

PEPPER, POTATO & CHORIZO TORTILLA

SERVES 2

You can play around with the tortilla filling: try substituting sliced bacon for the chorizo, using sweet potato instead of regular potatoes, or adding grated cheese. Eat hot or cold, on its own or with salad.

Valle de la Luna, Atacama

YOU NEED

- 2 tablespoons olive or vegetable oil (plus extra to fry)
- 1 small onion, thinly sliced
- 1 garlic clove, finely chopped
- 1 medium waxy potato, peeled, cut in half and very thinly sliced
- ½ red pepper, thinly sliced
- 8 slices chorizo, cut into quarters
- ½ teaspoon paprika
- 4 large eggs
- 1 tablespoon milk
- 1 tablespoon finely chopped parsley or coriander (optional)
- Salt and black pepper

HOW

- Heat the oil in a non-stick frying pan, add the onion and garlic and fry until translucent.
- Add the sliced potato and pepper and cook until soft.
- Stir in the chorizo and paprika and cook for a minute or so before scooping everything on to a plate.
- Beat the eggs and milk together in a largish bowl, season with salt and pepper to taste and stir in the cooked vegetable/chorizo mixture and the chopped parsley until well combined.
- Wash and dry the frying pan, add a splash of oil and heat until the oil is really hot.
- Pour in the egg mixture, reduce the heat and continue to cook until the tortilla becomes golden brown underneath and just set in the middle.
- To turn the tortilla, place a large plate over the pan and flip the tortilla on to the plate.
- Add another drizzle of oil to the pan and when hot slip the tortilla from the plate back into the pan.
- Cook until golden brown, then turn off the heat and allow the tortilla to sit for a few minutes before cutting into wedges.

STREET STALL AUTHENTIC

Add a handful of 'value' small prawns along with the chorizo.

VEGETARIAN?

Skip the chorizo and add a small handful of grated cheese to the egg mixture.

THE COMPLETO HOT DOG

MAKES 2

There is a fine art to making a completo, Chile's beloved hot dog brimming with crushed avocado, tomato and mayonnaise.

YOU NEED

- 2 large frankfurters
- 1 large ripe avocado, diced
- 2 medium tomatoes, diced
- 2 spring onions, thinly sliced
- 2 large hot dog buns
- Mustard to taste
- 2 tablespoons mayonnaise
- A little chopped parsley (if you have it)
- Salt and black pepper

VEGETARIAN?

Use vegetarian frankfurters

HOW

- Place the frankfurters in a pan of gently simmering water and heat for 10 minutes, taking care not to boil the water as the frankfurters will split.
- Lightly crush the avocado with a fork, then stir in the chopped tomatoes, half the sliced spring onion and salt and pepper to taste.
- Cut the hot dog buns down the centre and smear the inside with mustard.
- Lay the frankfurter in the bun, cover with the avocado mixture and dollop the mayonnaise on top.
- Sprinkle with the remaining sliced spring onion and chopped parsley.

TANGO & STEAK IN ARGENTINA

After days roughing it in Argentina's great wide open, among unreal rainbow-coloured canyons, shifting glacial lakes, cacti-covered desert, lush jungles, roaring waterfalls and some of the Andes' most impressive peaks, it's time to spruce up for Buenos Aires street life, where tango and tortured tunes of love and loss fill the sidewalk. Catch up on culture, mooch around the vintage market and stroll through the crumbling crypts of Buenos Aires' atmospheric cemetery.

Take a tip from Argentina's gauchos and sip yerba mate tea from a gourd and gorge on the juiciest chargrilled steak you will ever taste in your life. Steak is a serious business here, cheap as chips and absolutely impossible to ignore. Vegetarians can seek solace in a plate of top-notch pasta, a legacy of Italian settlers.

THE PERFECT STEAK

PER STEAK

Parrilla steakhouses expertly cook every imaginable cut of beef to chargrilled perfection. I know, I know, steak is expensive back home. But when the bank balance will sustain it, treat yourself! After splashing out, you want to get it right. Timing is key — a steak can be ruined in minutes. Follow the instructions religiously for mouth-melting results. Then serve in the Argentinian way, with lashings of chimichurri sauce.

This recipe is for medium-rare steak, perfectly pink in the middle with a brown crust. Prefer it rare? Knock half a minute from the cooking time on each side. For medium, add half a minute. If you are cooking more than one steak, don't overload the pan. It's better to cook one at a time.

YOU NEED

- I room-temperature steak (approx. 2cm/¾ inch thick)
- Olive or sunflower oil
- Salt and pepper

HOW

- Rub or brush a thin coating of oil over the steak.
- Heat a heavy frying pan (or ridged griddle pan if you are lucky enough to have one) over a medium-high heat setting until it's smoking hot.
- Season the steak generously with salt and black pepper just before laying it in the hot pan.
- Press the steak into the pan with a spatula and cook for exactly 2 minutes before turning and cooking for a further 2 minutes. Remember to watch that clock!
- Whip it out of the pan and leave it to rest (i.e, don't cut it) for 3 minutes. It's worth the wait.

STREET STALL AUTHENTIC

Serve with baked potatoes, salad and chimichurri sauce. To make the sauce, mix a small handful of finely chopped parsley with a tablespoon of grated onion, a crushed garlic clove, and a couple of tablespoons each of olive oil and red wine vinegar (or lemon juice). Season with ground chilli, salt and black pepper to taste.

COOKING TIPS

Use rump steak. It has a firmer texture than sirloin or rib eye but it's less pricey and full of flavour. **Choose** a steak with a marbling (fine flecks) of fat.

PASTA WITH TUCO TOMATO SALSA

SERVES 2 HUNGRY PEOPLE

Pimp up pasta with this trad tomato sauce. The cooking time of the pasta will vary depending on what type you use — spaghetti or penne are a top choice. Follow the instructions on the packet and cast an eye over the cooking tips for pasta on page 13.

YOU NEED

- 2 tablespoons olive oil
- I smallish red onion, grated
- ½ pepper (any colour), grated
- I garlic clove, grated
- ½ teaspoon paprika
- Ix 400g/14oz tin chopped tomatoes
- 2 tablespoons tomato purée
- ½ teaspoon dried oregano
- 2 bay leaves
- ½ teaspoon brown sugar or honey
- A few basil leaves
- Salt and black pepper
- Cooked pasta of your choice
- Grated Parmesan cheese to serve

HOW

- Heat the olive oil in a saucepan, add the onion, pepper and garlic and stir-fry until the vegetables are just soft.
- Stir in the paprika and cook for a few seconds before adding the chopped tomatoes, tomato purée, oregano and sugar.
- Stir the sauce until the purée has dissolved, then cover the pan and gently simmer until it becomes rich, oily and reduced.
- Add the basil and season with salt and pepper to taste.
- Spoon generous scoops of sauce on to the hot cooked pasta of your choice. Sprinkle with grated cheese if you wish.

STREET STALL AUTHENTIC

Add a generous amount of dried chilli flakes at the same time as the paprika.

COOKING TIP

Customize your tuco sauce: add sliced mushrooms, diced aubergine or sliced spinach, or think of some ideas of your own.

LEFT Backpacking in Argentina

AFRICA OVERLAND

Cooking outside is a way of life in Africa: from the hunter gatherer one-pot stews concocted from beans, root vegetables and meat, simmered over an open fire in the bush, to the weekend institution of a lavish braai barbecue fuelled by crates of beer in the 'burbs'. Africa's history has created a cuisine of great contrasts, shaped by indigenous tribes, colonial invaders and exotic traders: it can be simple sustenance or full of spice.

Cornmeal porridge, the local staple that clocks up energy-giving carbs, is served either thin and sprinkled with sugar for breakfast or mashed-potato thick with a ladle of veg or meat stew at lunch and dinner. The porridge's name varies from country to country (mealie meal, ugali, nshima or sadza), and it is sometimes made with millet or cassava flour, but the dish is roughly the same. Stay overnight in a Maasai village and you can sample the real McCoy. In season termites and grasshoppers are added to the pot.

Colonial settlers imported cattle and sheep and a passion for grilled meat and biltong. Cuisine is unashamedly meaty and wild game is often on the menu: you can be snapping kudu or ostrich on safari in the afternoon and later chomping on it for supper. It's not the easiest destination for vegetarians, but wherever there's an Indian community you'll be well rewarded with veggie curries and spicy snacks.

Away from the gourmet sophistication of South Africa's urban café society and the fresh seafood coconut curry feasts of Zanzibar, culinary highs can be few and far between on an overland trip through Africa. However, if you know where to look there are always treats to be found along the way. For instance, in small town Namibia look out for German bakeries serving fresh brotchen, pizza and pastries, to be washed down with steaming cups of strong coffee, and cafés serving wholesome stews. The beer ain't bad either. Local breweries churn out bottles of thirst-quenching lager-style beer, always best served icy cold at sundown around the camp fire after a dusty day on the road.

CLOCKWISE FROM TOP LEFT
Beach, Zanzibar; Victoria Falls, Zambia;
Dancing Samburu warriors, East Africa;
Stone Town pilau (see page 80); an elephant
in South Luangwa National Park, Zambia

THE AFRICAN STORE CUPBOARD

African ingredients are quite straightforward. Apart from garlic, ginger root, chilli and a jar of sweet chutney, you just need a few extra spices, all easy to find in supermarkets or local ethnic stores.

Curry powder: Some curry powders are better than others. Read the ingredients list and choose the one with the longest list of spices. Available from mild to hot, medium is a safe bet.

Ground mixed spice: A blend of sweet spices often used in baking. The dominant ingredients are cinnamon, nutmeg and allspice, the spices added to Namibian potje.

Garam masala: A combination of spices that normally includes cloves, cumin, cinnamon, cardamom and black pepper. It gives an instant injection of aromatic spice.

Bay leaves

Tinned tomatoes and tomato purée

Chutney: A spoonful of spiced sweet chutney is often mixed into recipes — mango, apple and apricot work best.

Rice: Long-grain white rice is typical, but you can also use brown.

TUCKING IN
UNDER TABLE MOUNTAIN

Cosmopolitan Cape Town fires the spirit of adventurein more ways than one. Revel in the bird's-eye view from a cable car, high above the city bowl, as it clanks its way to the top of Table Mountain. Trek the rocky trail to the bottom, or take the once-in-a-lifetime challenge and abseil back down. Party hard with copious Karate Water cocktails in Long Street, or dip your toe in the relaxed surfer scene on Cape Town's golden sands. If you dare to see what lurks beneath the water, swimming with sharks is a real experience — but you might find watching jackass penguins waddling on the Cape less hair-raising. For a sobering reminder of South Africa's relatively recent past, visit Nelson Mandela's prison cell on Robben Island.

To get under the skin of the foodie scene, share a 'local dinner' with a family in their home. It's a real insight into how multi-cultural migration has influenced the South African appetite.

View of Cape Town from Table Mountain

BOBOTIE

SERVES 2 (or multiply for more mouths)

This Cape Malay one-dish recipe is South Africa's favourite comfort food, served up with yellow rice and thick slices of tomato topped with slivers of onion and chilli. It's a brilliant meal if you are expecting a crowd round.

YOU NEED

- A small heat-proof dish
- 1 thick slice white bread
- 150ml/1/4 pint full fat milk
- 1 dessertspoon vegetable oil
- 250g/9oz beef mince
- 1 tablespoon butter
- 1 small onion, diced
- 1 garlic clove, crushed
- 1 heaped teaspoon medium curry powder
- ½ teaspoon dried mixed herbs
- 1 tablespoon mango chutney
- 1 tablespoon raisins
- 1 large egg, beaten
- Salt and black pepper

STREET STALL AUTHENTIC

Lay a bay leaf on top of the egg mixture just before placing the dish in the oven.
Serve topped with slices of banana.

VEGETARIAN?
Use a vegetarian mince replacement or an equal quantity of drained tinned lentils.

HOW

- Preheat the oven to 180C/350F/gas mark 4
- Place the bread in a bowl and pour the milk over the top.
- Leave the bread to soak while you prepare the meat.
- Heat the vegetable oil in a frying pan, add the mince and cook (breaking up any clumps with a wooden spoon) until the meat is brown. Remove the meat from the pan and set to one side.
- Melt the butter in the same pan, add the onion and garlic and fry until soft.
- Stir in the curry powder and mixed herbs and stir-fry for 1 minute before returning the browned meat to the pan.
- Add the chutney, a couple of tablespoons of water and salt and black pepper to taste.
- Cover the pan and simmer for 5 minutes (stirring regularly to stop the meat sticking).
- Squeeze the bread to remove any excess milk — keep the milk — and stir the bread mush into the meat mixture.
- Whisk the reserved milk with the egg and season with salt and black pepper to taste.
- Tip the meat into a small heat-proof dish, press it down into the dish with the back of a spoon and flatten the top.
- Pour the egg mixture over the top. Place on the middle shelf of the preheated oven and bake for 30 minutes — if you're making a larger amount bake for 35–40 minutes — until the topping is golden brown and the egg has set.

SERVE

With yellow rice: fry 1 tablespoon of raisins and a good pinch of turmeric for a few seconds in a knob of butter before adding the rice and cooking in the normal way (see page 13).

BUNNY CHOW

SERVES 2

After a day on the beach nothing quite beats a 'bunny', South Africa's answer to fast food invented by the Indian community of Durban as a convenient way to transport a curry lunch. The dough from half a white loaf is scooped out to leave the crust and the cavity is filled with curry. Large crusty rolls are much easier to handle and classier to look at. The curry is traditionally veggie but you can add diced chicken or mince.

YOU NEED

- 2 large round crusty bread rolls
- 2 tablespoons vegetable oil
- I small onion, diced
- I garlic clove, crushed
- 2cm/¾ inch piece ginger root, peeled and finely chopped, or I dessertspoon puréed bottled ginger
- I medium carrot, diced
- I medium potato, peeled and diced
- A handful of diced butternut squash or cauliflower broken into florets (or diced chicken or mince)
- I heaped teaspoon curry powder
- ½ a 400g/14oz tin chopped tomatoes
- ⅓ a 400g/14oz tin chickpeas (or other tinned beans), drained
- 110ml/4fl oz water
- I teaspoon garam masala
- Salt and black pepper to taste

STREET STALL AUTHENTIC

Serve with a handful of grated carrot dressed with a squeeze of lemon juice and finely chopped chilli and salt to taste.

COOKING TIP

Top the curry with a spoonful of natural yoghurt before covering with the bread lid.

HOW

- Cut the tops off the bread rolls — save the tops to make a small lid for the bunny — and scoop out the doughy centre to make a bread 'bowl', leaving a layer of bread lining the crust to soak up the curry sauce.
- Heat the oil in a thick-bottomed saucepan and fry the onion, garlic and ginger until soft.
- Add the vegetables and stir-fry until they start to soften (or add meat and fry until browned).
- Stir in the curry powder, stir-fry for 1 minute, then add the chopped tomatoes, chickpeas and water. Give the pan a good stir and bring the bunny to the boil.
- Reduce the heat to a simmer, cover the pan and continue to cook until the vegetables are soft.
- Stir in the garam masala, season with salt and black pepper to taste.
- Fill the bread bowls with curry and cover with the cut-bread lids.

SUPPER UNDER THE STARS IN NAMIBIA

The diversity of Namibia's vast landscapes ensures it is one of the greatest road journeys in the world. Climb the carved ridges of picture-perfect golden dunes, feel the heat in the oldest desert known to man, spot the 'big five' in the blissfully uncrowded Etosha wildlife park and the lush wetlands of the Caprivi Strip, be moved by the haunting beauty of the Skeleton Coast and feel at peace in the endless plains of the interior.

Cuisine is a mix of tribal and German colonial cooking. Meaty braii barbecues and spiced stews slowly simmered in a cast-iron cauldron over an open fire are guaranteed to be served under a star-filled night sky in a land free of light pollution. The German tradition of baking is also a bonus. Local coffee shops serve fresh bread, apple strudel and scrumptious cakes.

Caprivi Strip, Namibia

BEANY CHAKALAKA

SERVES 2

Top this veggie curried bean stew with grated cheese or an avocado dip and serve with crusty bread, rice or mash. Non veggies missing meat can fry up some sausages to go with it.

YOU NEED

- I tablespoon vegetable oil
- ½ medium onion, diced
- I garlic clove, finely chopped
- Icm/½ inch ginger root, peeled and grated, or I teaspoon puréed bottled ginger
- I red chilli, thinly sliced (or ground chilli to taste)
- ½ medium green pepper, diced
- ½ medium red pepper, diced
- I heaped teaspoon curry powder
- I large carrot, grated
- ½ a 400g/14oz tin chopped tomatoes
- ½ a 400g/14oz tin baked beans
- I heaped teaspoon tomato purée
- 2 bay leaves
- Salt and black pepper

HOW

- Heat the oil in a thick-bottomed saucepan, add the onion, garlic, ginger, chilli and pepper and stir-fry until soft.
- Add the grated carrot, cook for a couple more minutes, then stir in the curry powder.
- Add the tomatoes, baked beans, tomato purée, bay leaves and 4 tablespoons of water.
- Season with salt and pepper to taste and gently simmer, stirring every once in a while, for a further 10 minutes or so until the sauce has thickened.

STREET STALL AUTHENTIC

Spice it up with extra chopped chilli.

SERVE

With avocado dip: mash a small ripe avocado with a couple of tablespoons of cream cheese and natural yoghurt, finely chopped chilli (or a sprinkling of ground chilli) to taste and a squeeze of lemon juice.

CHICKEN POTJE

SERVES 2

A good one for the slow cooker. Not quite as romantic as a cast-iron three-legged pot suspended over a fire but just as welcome after a long day.

YOU NEED

- I tablespoon vegetable oil
- 4 chicken drumsticks, seasoned with salt
- ½ medium onion, sliced
- I garlic clove, finely chopped
- 2 medium carrots, thick sliced on a diagonal
- I medium potato, peeled and thick sliced
- I teaspoon ground mixed spice
- ¼ teaspoon ground black pepper
- I tablespoon mango or apple chutney
- 110ml/4fl oz hot chicken or vegetable stock
- Salt

HOW

- Heat the oil in a frying pan and brown the chicken drumsticks on all sides.
- Place the drumsticks in the bottom of the slow cooker dish and sprinkle with the onion, garlic and a third of the mixed spice.
- Cover with a layer of sliced carrot and potato, sprinkling each layer with the remaining mixed spice, pepper and salt to taste.
- Stir the chutney into the hot stock and pour the mixture evenly over the top.
- Following the maker's instructions, cook the potje on either the fast or slow setting (depending on how soon you want the stew to be ready).

STREET STALL AUTHENTIC

Add a quarter of a teaspoon of ground turmeric and 2 bay leaves at the same time as the mixed spice.

74

NO SLOW COOKER?

Layer the stew in a heavy-bottomed saucepan (with a lid), and increase the quantity of stock to 150ml/5fl oz. Cover the pan and simmer for an hour or so over a low heat until the chicken is cooked through.

VEGETARIAN?

Replace the chicken with layers of thick-sliced sweet potato, butternut squash and red pepper, and reduce the cooking time as listed in the maker's instructions. Alternatively, cook in a covered saucepan over a low heat until the vegetables are soft. (Expect this to take approximately 30–35 minutes.)

BUSH CAMP COOKING ON THE ZAMBEZI

Get the adrenalin pumping and the heart pounding at the thundering Victoria Falls, the largest waterfall in the world. Take the 'total challenge' with a bungee jump, 'swing' and 'slide' and a white-knuckle water-rafting ride. Swim to the edge of the falls, just before it crashes miles below, or scream and shout in its soaking spray. Canoeing on the Zambezi is a much calmer pursuit and offers the chance to eyeball hefty hippos, dozing crocs and majestic elephants at close hand.

Chillax at the end of the day with a local beer and spicy barbecued chicken on board a sunset cruise, drifting along the serene Zambezi while watching wildlife take their refreshment from the river in the cool of the setting sun.

Victoria Falls, Zambia

CHILLI & GARLIC BARBECUE SAUCE

MAKES 110ML/4FL OZ (enough for a few meals — unless you tend to be heavy handed with chilli!)

This BBQ sauce is drizzled over all manner of grilled meat, even crocodile. Back home opt for anything from chicken to fish fillets, or break away from the meat fest with thick slices of veggie Indian paneer cheese or halloumi. Serve whatever you choose with rice, any green veg or salad.

YOU NEED

- I tablespoon very finely chopped red chilli (seeds removed)
- I fat garlic clove, finely chopped
- I dessertspoon vegetable oil
- 2 tablespoons lemon juice
- 3 tablespoons olive oil
- ¼ teaspoon salt

HOW

- Fry the chopped chilli and garlic in the vegetable oil until soft and golden.
- Whisk the remaining ingredients together until the salt has dissolved and stir in the fried chilli and garlic.

STREET STALL AUTHENTIC

Use two tablespoons of hot red chillies.

COOKING TIP

Use mild chillies if hot chilli leaves you cold. **Coat** the meat, fish or veggie option of your choice with the sauce and cook under the grill or on a barbie — you can even fry it — until chargrilled on the outside and cooked in the middle. Spoon extra sauce to taste over the top.

FRIED FISH WITH GREENS & TOMATO RELISH

SERVES 2

Tiger fish is traditionally served with this tomatoey relish but any reasonably priced white fish will do. Cornmeal porridge normally soaks up the sauce. It's probably not top of your travel recipe take-home list so serve with buttery mashed potato instead.

YOU NEED

- 2 fillets white fish
- 1 large knob of butter
- 2 tablespoons vegetable oil
- ½ medium onion, peeled and diced
- 1 garlic clove, crushed
- A handful of thinly sliced spinach or chard

- ½ a 400g/14oz tin chopped tomatoes
- ½ teaspoon sugar
- A squeeze of lemon juice
- Salt and black pepper

HOW

- Heat the oil in a frying pan, add the onion and garlic and cook until soft.
- Add the sliced greens and stir-fry until the greens start to wilt.
- Add the chopped tomatoes and sugar, cover the pan and simmer until the sauce has reduced and the greens are cooked.
- Add a squeeze of lemon juice and season with salt and ground black pepper to taste.
- Season the fish fillets with salt and fry in the butter until the fish is golden brown and cooked through.
- Pop the fish on to a plate and spoon the relish over the top.

STREET STALL AUTHENTIC

Stir a heaped tablespoon of crushed raw peanuts into the cooked relish.

VEGETARIAN?

Replace the fish with thick slices of halloumi cheese.

SPICING IT UP IN TANZANIA

Go on safari in Tanzania's sweeping savannah. Track the rare black rhino deep inside the crater of an extinct volcanic at Ngorongoro and follow big cats licking their lips and dreaming of supper as they stalk herds of wildebeest on the wide-open plains of the Serengeti. Jump high with the Maasai at Lake Manyara and see if you've got what it takes to climb the challenging glacial summit of Mount Kilimanjaro. Kick off the walking boots on one of Zanzibar's postcard perfect palm-fringed coves, cruise the crystal coastal waters under the billowing sail of an Arab dhow and dive deep to coral reefs teeming with fish.

Cooking is quite varied. In mainland Tanzania barbecued goat and meat stews provide sustenance without sophistication, whereas the coastal strip has the flavours added by sea traders, a melting pot of African, Arab and Indian cooking that is well worth recreating.

A fish market, Dar es Salaam, Tanzania

STONE TOWN PILAU

SERVES 2

YOU NEED

- 2 tablespoons vegetable oil
- 250g/9oz diced chicken (or lamb)
- I small onion, diced
- ½ smallish green pepper, diced
- I medium waxy potato, peeled and cubed
- 2 garlic cloves, finely chopped
- 2cm/¾ inch ginger root, peeled and grated or dessertspoon bottled puréed ginger
- I heaped teaspoon garam masala
- I green chill, slit lengthwise
- I medium tomato, diced
- 2 tablespoons sultanas
- ½ mug white basmati rice
- I mug hot chicken or vegetable stock
- Salt and ground black pepper to taste

HOW

- Heat I tablespoon of the oil in a heavy bottomed saucepan (with a fitted lid), add the meat and stir-fry until browned on all sides.
- Scoop the meat on to a spare plate and add the remaining oil to the pan.
- Add the onion, garlic and ginger and stir-fry until soft.
- Add the pepper and potato and continue to cook for a few minutes until the vegetables start to soften.
- Stir in the garam masala and rice and when everything is well coated with spice add the chicken, chopped tomato, raisins and chilli.
- Pour in the stock and season with salt and black pepper to taste.
- Bring the pan to a simmer, cover with a lid and continue to cook until all the stock has been absorbed (expect this stage to take about 10 minutes, although cooking time will vary slightly depending on your cooker).
- Turn the heat off and leave the pilau to sit with the lid on for 5 minutes.
- Fluff the pilau with a fork and spoon on to plates.

VEGETARIAN?
Replace the meat with a small tin of drained chickpeas or mixed beans.

HUNGRY?
Make the salad more of a main meal by adding a small tin of drained kidney beans to the mixture, pile on to a bed of mixed leaves and top with scoops of soft goat's cheese or cream cheese.

CACHUMBA SALAD

SERVES 2
AS A SIDE SALAD

YOU NEED
- Cucumber, roughly 13cm/ 5 inch, cut in half lengthwise
- 3 medium tomatoes, cut in half
- 3 spring onions, sliced
- Juice of ½ small lemon
- A small handful of coriander leaves
- ¼ teaspoon ground cumin
- Salt and black pepper to taste

HOW
- Scoop away the seeds from the cucumber and tomatoes with a spoon and dice the remaining flesh.
- Place the diced cucumber and tomatoes in a bowl and mix with the remaining ingredients until well combined.

FIND YOURSELF IN INDIA

Buckle your seat belt for the culinary experience of a lifetime! India's food is as diverse as the subcontinent itself and as colourful as a careering tuk-tuk ride through its cities' teeming streets. There are inevitably going to be love or loathe moments when you are just as likely to be infuriated by the cuisine as you are infatuated. Snacking is obligatory and the buzzing street food scene an institution. It's easy to eat breakfast, lunch and dinner without taking a seat at a restaurant table. Samosas and chilli pakoras are served piping hot, straight from a cauldron of boiling oil, paper-thin dosas, stuffed parathas and masala omelettes are adeptly assembled on a massive cast-iron tawa, and creamy thick lassi churned in a wooden pestle and mortar — all with a flourish.

In the home, preparing the daily meal is a labour of love. A good part of the day is spent cooking: pounding garlic, ginger, onion and chilli and grinding a careful balance of whole spices to mix the family's secret masala spice recipe. Fill-up thali restaurants are the places to eat if you're hungry. Curries, dal, raita, chutney, rice and bread are served on a huge steel plate or banana leaf and constantly replenished until you can't possibly eat any more — you even get pudding!

Each state has its own style and speciality. In the north dishes are rich and highly spiced, just the way the maharajas and Mughals liked them, and in the palm-covered south, coconut is always in there somewhere. Cooking styles have been handed down through the centuries and what and how people eat is still inextricably linked with the traditions of India's major faiths. The best advice is to embrace it all wholeheartedly, and on the days when you really can't face another curry take a break with a cheesy toastie or a mild biryani and start again.

CLOCKWISE FROM BELOW Jawai Leopard Camp,
Rajasthan; street stall selling dosas in Hyderabad;
making sweets, Hyderabad; a village bazaar,
Rajasthan; Bhangarh, Rajasthan

THE INDIAN STORE CUPBOARD

The Indian store cupboard is all about spice. Having a good selection to hand makes recreating recipes easy. This doesn't need to be expensive. Just buy them in an Asian store. To keep flavours fresh, store open spice packets in jam jars with tight-fitting lids. When cooking with spices, always make sure the oil is nice and hot. Whole spices are generally added first — stand back a little, the seeds will crackle and pop in the hot oil. Ground spices need to be kept on the move in the pan or they tend to stick and burn. The combination of onion, garlic, ginger and chilli forms the base to most dishes.

Spices: Ground turmeric (take care - it stains everything it touches), ground cumin, ground coriander, garam masala, mustard seeds, cumin seeds, ground chilli, and (not so essential) ground cardamom and cinnamon.

Ginger/garlic: Fresh is best or you can buy them puréed in a jar.

Fresh chillies

Fresh coriander

Curry paste: Sold in jars: choose from mild to hot.

Red split lentils

Tinned chickpeas

Tinned coconut milk

Mango chutney

Rice: Basmati is best but it's a little more expensive than long grain.

Chapatis or naan: Unleavened flat bread (sold in packets), a super-speedy alternative to rice.

Curry leaves: This one is for dedicated foodies, well worth searching out if you have a good Asian store nearby.

CAMEL-TREKKING IN RAJASTHAN

This is desert country. Women clad in multicoloured saris and men sporting vivid turbans and sculpted moustaches herd lolloping cattle and wayward goats into the dusty horizon. Fantasy palaces and hilltop forts of the warrior Rajputs offer a lingering reminder of an opulent past, and nomadic tribal people lead their camel trains through candy-painted villages. In the towns, a maze of narrow streets squeezes through temples, havelis and treasure-trove shops.

Escape the hustle and bustle on a camel safari, the only way to arrive at the sandcastle-like citadel of Jaisalmer. Growing produce successfully under the fierce midday sun isn't easy. Rajasthanis rely on grains, dried pulses, milk, eggs, desert beans and vegetables from the bazaar or the backyard.

Goat herder, Rajasthan

DESERT DAL

SERVES 2

Low in calories, high in protein, full of flavour and ridiculously cheap to make. What more can you ask for? Serve with rice and yoghurt raita.

YOU NEED

- ¾ mug red split lentils
- 3 tablespoons vegetable oil
- 1 teaspoon cumin seeds
- 1 teaspoon mustard seeds
- 1 medium onion, diced
- 4cm/1½ inch piece ginger root, peeled and finely chopped, or 1 tablespoon bottled puréed ginger
- 2 garlic cloves, finely chopped
- ½ teaspoon ground turmeric
- 2 handfuls of young leaf spinach, thinly sliced

HOW

- Rinse the lentils in cold water until the water runs clear. Set to one side for later.
- Heat the oil in a medium-size saucepan and when hot add the mustard and cumin seeds.
- As the seeds start to pop, add the onion, ginger and garlic and cook until soft.
- Stir in the turmeric, followed by the rinsed lentils and 2 mugs of cold water.
- Bring the pan to the boil (skimming away any foam that rises to the top), then reduce the heat and gently simmer until the lentils break down.
- Add the sliced spinach and salt to taste and continue to cook until the spinach is soft.

STREET STALL AUTHENTIC

Fry sliced chilli with the onion, ginger and garlic mixture.
Sprinkle the dal with chopped coriander.
Add a good pinch of ground cumin to the raita.

COOKING TIP

Add a selection of your favourite diced vegetables at the same time as the lentils as an alternative to spinach.

YOGHURT RAITA

SERVES 2

Cool the effects of hot chillies with this minty yoghurt raita.

YOU NEED

- 1 small pot natural yoghurt
- 5cm/2 inch piece cucumber, finely diced
- 1 heaped dessertspoon finely chopped mint leaves
- Salt to taste

HOW

- Scoop the yoghurt into a bowl and whisk with a fork until smooth.
- Stir in the remaining ingredients and season with salt to taste.

FRUITY OPTIONS

Use diced ripe mango instead of cucumber

TIFFIN AT THE TAJ MAHAL

Agra is a touristy kind of place, but you can't go to India without seeing the Taj Mahal. Built by the doomed Shah Jahan as a lasting tribute to his beloved wife Mumtaz, the white domes and spires of this monument of love glimmer in the shimmering sun like a mirage. Be there at sunrise with the crowds and share a group-hug moment as its beauty is revealed — don't be surprised to hear audible gasps. It certainly lives up to its 'wonder of the world' tag. In town, rooftop restaurants offer Western-friendly Indian dishes and cheesy comfort food with a twist, and a tantalizing glimpse of 'that' view.

Taj Mahal, Agra

CHEESE & TOMATO JAYFELLES

PER SANDWICH

Decadently cheesy toasties, best enjoyed with a creamy banana lassi. A toastie machine is definitely an advantage for making jayfelles, but a frying pan also does the trick.

YOU NEED

- 2 slices medium-cut bread
- Soft butter to spread and extra to cook
- 75g/3oz Cheddar cheese, grated
- 1 tablespoon finely chopped red onion
- 1 dessertspoon chopped coriander
- 1 tablespoon mango chutney
- 4 tomato slices

HOW

- Thinly butter both sides of the sliced bread and mix the grated cheese with the chopped red onion and coriander.
- Spread one slice of the buttered bread with mango chutney, sprinkle with the cheese mixture and lay the tomato slices on top. Cover with the remaining bread and gently press together to make a sandwich.
- Melt a nob of butter in a frying pan, lay the sandwich in the pan, and cook over a low to medium heat for approximately 1½ minutes on each side, until the cheese is molten and the bread golden brown.
- If you are using a toastie maker, pop the prepared sandwich in the machine and cook following the maker's instructions.

STREET STALL AUTHENTIC

Add chopped chilli and a small handful of sprouted mung beans to the cheese.

BANANA LASSI

MAKES 2 BIG GLASSES

A food processor or stick blender is
handy to make smooth, frothy lassi.
In a more basic kitchen, a fork or whisk
does the job, as long as the banana
is well mashed.

YOU NEED

- 1 medium ripe banana, peeled and
  mashed to a pulp with a fork or
  potato masher
- 175g/6oz natural yoghurt
- 200ml/7fl oz chilled milk
- 1 teaspoon honey
- A good pinch of ground cardamom

HOW

- Whizz all the ingredients in a food
  processor (or place in a
  bowl and whisk together)
  until smooth and frothy.

STREET STALL AUTHENTIC

Add a tablespoon of
rose water.

NO BANANAS?

Add a generous pinch of salt to
make salt lassi or extra honey
to taste for sweet.
Use crushed berries instead
of banana.

GRAZING AT THE GHATS IN VARANASI

Join the never-ending stream of Hindu pilgrims that flock in droves to the holy city of Varanasi. It's an eye-opening experience and not for everyone. Sights and smells will be etched on your memory forever. All life (and death) is played out on the temple-lined ghats that lead to the banks of the sacred River Ganges. People come to bathe, perform puja, practise yoga, meditate, take a boat ride and cremate their dead. At night the ghats burn bright with the firelight of the ganga aarti river-worshipping ceremony, the air thick with incense and the sound of chanting, and the dark waters of the river decorated with streams of bobbing butter lamps floating on its surface. Leave the ghats at your peril: the maze of narrow alleyways beyond them is easy to get lost in and you are bound to bump into stray cows blocking your path and funeral processions making their way to the river.

STREET STALL AUTHENTIC

Add a squeeze of lemon juice and chopped mint leaves to serve.

VEGETARIAN?

Replace the chicken with a handful of bite-size cauliflower florets and diced butternut squash.

EASY BIRYANI

SERVES 2

At rooftop cafés overlooking the wide sweep of the Ganges, biryanis are a firm favourite with travellers. A traditional biryani can take hours to prepare. This recipe keeps it simple.

YOU NEED

- ²/₃ mug basmati rice
- 1 rounded tablespoon butter
- 1 medium onion, thinly sliced
- 1 garlic clove, finely chopped
- 1 teaspoon garam masala
- ¼ teaspoon ground turmeric
- Ground chilli to taste
- 2 skinless chicken breasts, diced
- 7 dried apricots, chopped
- 1 tablespoon curry paste
- 3 tablespoons natural yoghurt
- 1½ mugs hot chicken (or vegetable) stock
- A small bunch of chopped coriander
- 2 heaped tablespoons cashew nuts
- Salt and black pepper to taste

HOW

- Wash rice in cold water until the water runs clear, tip off any excess water and set aside.
- Melt the butter in a medium-size saucepan, add the onion and garlic and fry until soft.
- Stir in the garam masala, turmeric and chilli to taste, cook for a few seconds, then add the chicken and apricots.
- Stir-fry until the chicken is well coated in spice and starting to brown.
- Add the rice, curry paste and yoghurt, give the pan a stir, then pour in the stock and season with salt and pepper to taste.
- Bring the pan to the boil, then reduce the heat to a simmer, cover the pan and continue to cook until all the stock has been absorbed.
- Turn off the heat and leave the covered pan to sit for 10 minutes before fluffing the biryani with a fork.
- Stir in the chopped coriander and scatter with the cashew nuts before serving.

LEFT Varanasi

STORE CUPBOARD VEGETABLE CURRY

SERVES 2

In the holy city of Varanasi, vegetarian curries are top of the menu. When the fridge is empty, this instant vegetable curry can be cooked with a few store-cupboard staples. Serve with rice and a spoonful of mango chutney.

STREET STALL AUTHENTIC

Add a handful of finely chopped coriander stalks at the same time as the ground spices.

YOU NEED

- 2 tablespoons vegetable oil
- ½ teaspoon cumin seeds
- ½ teaspoon mustard seeds
- 1 medium onion, thinly sliced
- 2 garlic cloves, chopped
- 2cm/¾ inch piece ginger root, peeled and chopped, or 1 dessertspoon bottled puréed ginger
- ½ teaspoon turmeric
- 1 teaspoon garam masala

- Ground chilli to taste
- ½ mug tinned sweetcorn
- ½ mug tinned chickpeas
- ½ mug frozen peas or frozen chopped spinach
- ½ a 400g/14oz tin chopped tomatoes
- ¼ mug water
- 1 teaspoon honey
- Salt

HOW

- Heat the oil in a medium-size saucepan. When the oil is really hot, add the cumin and mustard seeds.
- Let the seeds crackle and pop for a few seconds before adding the sliced onion, garlic and ginger.
- Continue to cook, stirring constantly, until the onions are soft and caramelized.
- Stir in the turmeric, garam masala and chilli until the onions are well coated in spice.
- Add the sweetcorn, chickpeas and peas (or spinach), give the pan a good stir and cook for a further minute before adding the chopped tomatoes, water, honey and salt to taste.
- Bring the curry to a gentle simmer and continue to cook until the vegetables are cooked and the sauce has reduced a little.

COOKING TIP

Cook double the quantity — it tastes even better the next day.
Add 2 halved hard-boiled eggs to the curry five minutes before the end of the cooking time.

BRUNCH ON THE BACKWATERS OF KERALA

Forget about life on land for a while and doze on board the deck of a thatched houseboat as it drifts through the coconut-palm-fringed canals and lagoons of Kerala's lush backwaters. Watch day to day Keralan life paddle by along the sleepy waterways that operate as a freeway for locals. Everything is transported by boat, from cows to coconuts, and it makes very entertaining viewing from the comfort of a rattan chair. Wave to laughing children on the distant shore, take a dip in the lagoon, stop at tiny villages and savour creamy coconut curries flavoured with spices from Kerala's Cardamom Hills.

Houseboat, Kerala

VEGETARIAN?

Swap the fish for chunks of paneer cheese fried in oil until golden and a teacup of frozen peas.

SEAFOOD MOLÉE

SERVES 2

STREET STALL AUTHENTIC

Fry 8 curry leaves along with the mustard seeds.

Keralan home-style cooking isn't as difficult as you might think. Once the ingredients are assembled, seafood molee is very quick to make. You can use any firm white fish, or prawns. Serve with naan bread or rice.

YOU NEED

- 2 tablespoons vegetable oil
- I teaspoon mustard seeds
- I smallish onion, thinly sliced
- 2 garlic cloves, finely chopped
- 2cm/¾ inch piece ginger root, peeled and finely chopped, or I dessertspoon bottled puréed ginger
- Sliced green chillies to taste

- ½ teaspoon turmeric
- ½ teaspoon garam masala
- 200ml/7fl oz thick coconut milk
- 2 skinless fish fillets, cut into big chunks (or 200g/7oz prawns)
- 2 small tomatoes, cut into quarters
- A squeeze of lemon juice
- Salt

HOW

- Heat the oil in a wok or frying pan and when hot add the mustard seeds.
- As the seeds start to pop, add the onion, garlic, ginger and chilli , and stir-fry the mixture until soft but not brown.
- Stir in the turmeric and garam masala, followed by half the coconut milk and an equal quantity of warm water. Season with salt to taste and heat over a medium heat until the sauce reaches a gentle simmer (do not boil).
- Add the chunks of fish and continue to simmer for 5 minutes before adding the tomato, the remaining coconut milk and a good squeeze of lemon juice.
- Gently simmer for a further 5 minutes until the tomatoes are cooked but not breaking down.

MASALA CHEESE OMELETTE
PER OMELETTE

A super-quick filler to rustle up for brunch or supper. If chillies leave you cold (or too hot), use finely chopped red pepper instead.

YOU NEED

- 2 large eggs
- 1 tablespoon milk
- A good pinch of black pepper
- A handful of grated cheese
- 2 spring onions, thinly sliced (or small handful of finely chopped onion)
- 1 small tomato, diced
- Sliced red chilli (or red pepper) to taste
- Tablespoon finely chopped coriander
- Salt
- 1 teaspoon butter to fry

HOW

- Beat the eggs, milk and black pepper together in a bowl until well combined.
- Stir in the cheese, spring onions, tomato, chilli, coriander and salt to taste.
- In a medium-size frying pan melt the butter over a high-ish temperature until it starts to foam.
- Swirl the melted butter around the pan and pour in the egg mixture.
- Cook the omelette until it is golden brown and set enough in the middle to flip over with a spatula.
- Cook for a further minute or so, then slip on to a plate.

STREET STALL AUTHENTIC

Add a ¼ teaspoon of ground cumin to the egg mixture
Serve with a big squirt of tomato ketchup.

COOKING TIP

Add a small handful of shredded spinach to pack in the greens.
Serve with chapati topped with melted cheese. Sprinkle grated cheese over the chapati and warm under a grill or in a frying pan until the cheese melts.

BAREFOOT IN THE BEACH SHACKS OF GOA

Recover from days on the road in the hedonist's haven of Goa. Blue skies, golden sandy beaches, crashing waves and lazy afternoons relaxing in a shady hammock soon soothe away the stress of long train and bus journeys. In the cool of the morning, cycle along empty beaches, past swaying coconut groves and rice paddy fields. When hunger pangs hit, take a few sandy steps to the nearest beach shack for a freshly caught seafood snack or a fiery vindaloo lunch.

As the moon rises, it's time to party under a star-filled sky. Tear yourself away from the beach for a cultural foray into the Portuguese quarters of Goa's capital Panjim or take in the sights and faded grandeur of Old Goa. Before heading on, cruise Anjuna's enormous hippy market for presents to take back home.

Beach shack, Goa

BEACHSIDE FISH FRY

SERVES 2

This classic Goan beach-shack fish fry works well with almost any fish. Alternatively, smear the paste on to prawns — the bigger the better for a splurge — or keep the budget real with a packet of small prawns. Serve with rice, any green veggies or salad.

YOU NEED

- 2 chunky fish fillets
- Vegetable oil to fry

MASALA SPICE PASTE
- I fat garlic clove, crushed
- 2cm/¾ inch piece ginger root, peeled and grated, or I dessertspoon puréed bottled ginger

- 2 teaspoon plain flour
- I flat teaspoon chilli powder (or to taste)
- ½ teaspoon ground cumin
- ¼ teaspoon turmeric
- A good pinch of black pepper
- 2 teaspoons lemon juice
- Salt to taste

HOW

- Mix the masala paste ingredients together in a small bowl until well combined.
- Slice shallow cuts in the fish at 2 cm/¾ inch intervals and coat with the masala paste.
- Heat a splash of oil in a frying pan and fry the fish on both sides over a medium heat until crunchy on the outside and cooked through the middle. (This will take approximately 3–4 minutes on each side, depending on the thickness of the fish.)

STREET STALL AUTHENTIC

Top with thinly sliced red onion mixed with finely chopped coriander and a squeeze of lemon juice.

VEGETARIAN?

Use thick slices of paneer cheese, halloumi or tofu.

BANANA PANCAKES

MAKES 4 THICK PANCAKES

Craving something sweet? Make a batch of these thick, fluffy pancakes sweetened with banana.

YOU NEED

- 110g/4oz plain flour
- 1 teaspoon baking powder
- 1 teaspoon sugar
- A good pinch of salt
- 1 medium egg, beaten
- 140ml/5fl oz whole milk
- 2 heaped tablespoons natural yoghurt
- 1 tablespoon melted butter
- 1 large ripe banana, crushed with a fork
- Butter to cook

HOW

- Combine the flour, baking powder, sugar and salt in a medium-size bowl.
- Whisk the milk, yoghurt and butter together in a separate bowl and gently stir into the flour mixture, crushing any lumps on the side of the bowl. Stir in the banana.
- Melt a knob of butter in a non-stick frying pan and ladle a quarter of the mixture into the pan.
- Cook over a low to medium heat until bubbles start to appear and the batter is set enough to be able to turn the pancake.
- Flip and continue to cook until the pancake is golden brown and cooked in the middle.

STREET STALL AUTHENTIC

Drizzle with warm runny honey.

COOKING TIP

Don't over beat the mixture or the pancakes will be heavy.

SOUTHEAST ASIA ON A SHOESTRING

Southeast Asian cookery is a wake-up call to the taste buds. There are obviously regional variations from country to country, but all offer a fine balance of salty, sour, sweet and spicy tastes mixed with spices and fresh herbs such as ginger, garlic, lemon grass, lime leaves, mint, chilli and coriander.

Fish sauce and fish paste provide the saltiness that is so popular in Southeast Asian cookery. This is pungent stuff and not always to Western tastes. If you're not a fan or prefer to keep a recipe vegetarian, soy sauce does the job. Lime juice or tamarind add sourness. These sharp flavours are softened by the addition of sweet palm sugar, made from sap collected from the Palmyra palm tree, its caramel sweetness easily replicated back home in brown sugar or honey. Spicy is pretty self-explanatory: chillies come in all shapes and sizes and strengths from mild to eye-watering. As a basic rule of thumb, small bird's-eye chillies tend to be the hottest while larger varieties add flavour without the burn.

The simple cafés and stalls clinging to the edge of street markets are the place to find truly authentic cooking at a fraction of the cost of tourist cafés. This is the real deal, where spicing is guaranteed not to be watered down to 'tourist tastes'. Zesty salads, fragrant curries, killer noodles and spicy soups are served family style, all at the same time, with a bowl of steaming rice, either white and fluffy or sticky and chewy.

The daily shop is a noisy social affair, catching up with the gossip almost as important as the main task of the day — cruising the market for the best-looking produce and haggling for the best possible price. Wandering around the market is an eye-opening experience. Everything that moves seems to be fair game — bugs and slithering fish, snails and unrecognizable meat — then suddenly among all the mêlée there is the familiar sight of soft croissants, pastries and crispy baguettes, remnants of a colonial culinary past that have become everyday favourites wherever the French have left their mark.

CLOCKWISE FROM TOP LEFT
Street food in Laos; Halong Bay, Vietnam; temple in Burma; street food in Burma; Siem Reap, Cambodia.

Southeast Asian ingredients are available from most large supermarkets, but Oriental stores sell a larger range and as well as being excellent value for money there is usually someone more than happy to give advice. Stock up on garlic, chillies, ginger, limes, and fresh basil and coriander. Ingredients such as lemon grass and lime leaves are always better fresh. Don't be put off by larger quantities — they freeze really well and will save you money in the long run. Suggestions for alternatives are also listed. Fish or soy sauce are in most recipes. As these are already quite salty, it's wise to taste everything before adding salt.

LEFT Farmers preparing rice paddies for planting, Chiang Mai, Thailand

THE SOUTHEAST ASIAN STORE CUPBOARD

Soy sauce: Available in dark and light options. If you don't want to invest in more than one type, dark soy sauce is the most versatile. Dilute with an equal quantity of water to create light soy sauce.

Fish sauce: A salty fishy sauce with a similar consistency to soy sauce.

Kecap manis: A sweet, thick soy sauce with a syrupy texture. If you find it hard to buy, go for the cheat's method and mix equal amounts of dark soy sauce and tomato ketchup.

Tins of coconut milk, bamboo shoots and straw mushrooms

Green curry and red curry paste: Stick to authentic Thai brands and store in the fridge once opened.

Oyster sauce: A thick, dark sauce flavoured with oyster essence. A vegetarian substitute for oyster sauce is also available, or you can use hoisin sauce.

Rice: Sticky rice is very authentic but jasmine and basmati rice are much easier to handle. Cheaper long-grain white rice is perfectly acceptable; brown makes a healthier option.

Rice noodles: Medium-thick flat noodles and thin vermicelli.

Ginger root: A knobbly root with a hot aftertaste. The fresh root keeps for quite a long time, or you can buy the spice puréed in a jar.

Lemon grass: A tough stalk with a distinct lemony flavour. Bashing the stalk along its length with a rolling pin before chopping releases extra flavour. At a push, thick strips of lemon rind can be used instead.

Lime leaves: Dark green leaves with a citrus scent, available fresh or dried. Cut away the central tough stem before adding to recipes. If you find lime leaves impossible to source, thick strips of lime zest make a good second best.

Peanuts: Skinless and unsalted.

Spices: Cinnamon sticks, star anise and turmeric.

THE COOKING SCHOOLS OF THAILAND

First port of call on the Southeast Asia circuit, and the ideal destination to acclimatize to the wonders and ways of the Orient, Thailand has it all: busy cities, idyllic beaches, hill-tribe trekking and infectiously friendly people. Most importantly, Thailand is incredibly user-friendly and relaxed, with just the right balance of home comfort and exoticism. Pause a while, get your bearings and sample some of the spicy, sweet and salty flavours that characterize Southeast Asian cooking.

A day at a cooking school is a brilliant introduction to the whys and ways of Thai cookery. A visit to the local food market is usually thrown in, a chance to sample ingredients and day-to-day life in the raw, and learn to decode the ins and outs of a Thai menu.

Beware! Thais love their food spicy, so make sure you use chilli to suit your level of tolerance.

A local market on the Thai-Burmese border

GREEN CURRY

SERVES 2

Take me back to the beach . . . green curry is so easy to make. All you need is a bona fide Thai green curry paste and a tin of coconut milk. Serve with rice or noodles.

YOU NEED

- I tablespoon sunflower oil
- I rounded dessertspoon Thai green curry paste
- 200g/7oz diced chicken, tofu or fish, or 175g/6oz raw prawns
- 75g/3oz green beans, topped and tailed and cut into chunks
- 110g/4oz bite-size broccoli florets
- 275ml/½ pint tinned coconut milk
- I dessertspoon fish sauce (or dark soy sauce)
- I teaspoon brown sugar or honey
- 3 thick strips of lime zest

HOW

- Heat the oil in a wok or saucepan, add the paste and stir-fry for I minute.
- Add the chicken, tofu or seafood and the prepared vegetables, and continue to stir-fry for a further minute.
- Stir in two-thirds of the coconut milk and quarter of a mug of water.
- Add the fish or soy sauce, sugar and lime zest.
- Gently simmer over a low heat until everything is cooked through and piping hot. (Remember chicken will need a longer cooking time than tofu or prawns. Test after 10 minutes.)
- Stir in the remaining coconut milk and simmer for a few minutes before serving.

STREET STALL AUTHENTIC

Use 3 lime leaves instead of lime zest. **Add** I stalk of lemon grass cut into 2cm/¾ inch pieces and a small handful of basil leaves.

COOKING TIPS

Swap the beans and broccoli for frozen peas or soybeans, baby sweetcorn cut in half lengthwise, halved button mushrooms (or a small tin of straw mushrooms), sugar-snap peas or mangetouts.

PAD THAI

SERVES 2

The unofficial national dish, sold everywhere from street stalls to beach cafés.

YOU NEED

- 175g/6oz medium-thick dried flat rice noodles
- 4 tablespoons natural unsalted peanuts

DRESSING
- 2 tablespoons fish sauce (or dark soy sauce)
- Juice of small lime
- 1 tablespoon brown sugar or honey
- 2 tablespoons vegetable oil
- ½ red onion, finely sliced
- 1 garlic clove, finely chopped
- 150g/6oz largish cooked prawns
- Ground chilli powder to taste
- 2 large eggs, lightly beaten
- 4 spring onions, sliced into 1cm/½ inch pieces
- 150g/6oz bean sprouts
- Lime wedges to serve

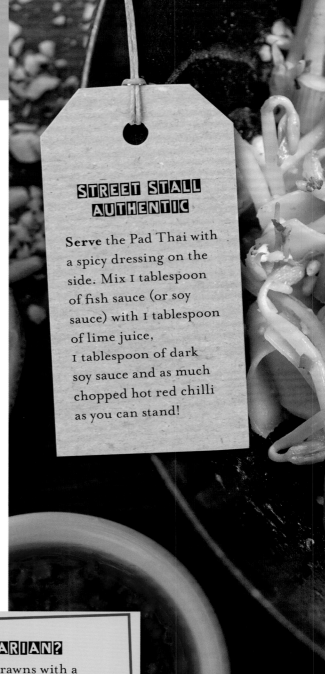

STREET STALL AUTHENTIC

Serve the Pad Thai with a spicy dressing on the side. Mix 1 tablespoon of fish sauce (or soy sauce) with 1 tablespoon of lime juice, 1 tablespoon of dark soy sauce and as much chopped hot red chilli as you can stand!

VEGETARIAN?
Replace prawns with a handful of diced firm tofu and use dark soy sauce instead of fish sauce.

HOW

- Cook the rice noodles as instructed on the packet.
- Drain the noodles and rinse with cold water, separating any that are stuck together.
- Dry roast the peanuts in a hot frying pan (no added oil) until they turn golden brown.
- Roughly chop the peanuts with a sharp knife (or crush with a rolling pin).
- Mix the dressing ingredients together until the sugar has dissolved.
- Heat the oil in a wok or large frying pan, add the red onion and garlic and fry until golden brown and soft.
- Add the ground chilli and cook for a few seconds.
- Add the prawns and stir-fry until they are heated through.
- Stir in the rinsed noodles, spring onions and bean sprouts.
- Add the dressing and stir-fry for a few minutes until everything is well coated.
- Make a well in the centre of the noodles, add the beaten egg and cook (stirring constantly) until the egg scrambles.
- Mix the scrambled egg into the noodles.
- Serve immediately, sprinkled with the chopped peanuts and a good squeeze of lime juice.

HAVEN'T GOT PRAWNS?

Use a skinless chicken breast cut into thin strips. If the chicken is uncooked, be sure to cook it through properly before adding the noodles.

113

MEALS ON THE MEKONG IN CAMBODIA

Cambodia sits deep in the heart of Indochina, a place of steamy jungles, tropical islands and ancient temples worthy of any wonder of the world. It offers traditional Khmer cooking mixed with a pinch of colonial French 'je ne sais quoi'. The good news for chilli-phobes is that, although Khmer cooking shares many similarities with Thai cuisine, Cambodians are much less fond of mouth-burning spice. Take time out to sip a tukalok (a kind of exotic fresh fruit smoothie) in one of the elegant pavement cafés of Phnom Penh, drift along the Mekong River to the wonderful temple complex of Angkor and savour Siem Reap's fantastic street food.

Angkor Wat, Cambodia

KHAO PHOUNE COCONUT RICE NOODLES

SERVES 2

A must-try Khmer one-bowl meal.

YOU NEED

- 110g/4oz dried rice vermicelli noodles (or 225g/8oz ready-cooked)
- 1 tablespoon vegetable oil
- 2 small chicken breasts, sliced
- 1 dessertspoon red curry paste
- 275ml/½ pint chicken or vegetable stock
- 200ml/7fl oz coconut milk
- 1 lemon grass stalk, cut into 2cm/¾ inch chunks, or 3 strips lemon rind
- 5 cherry tomatoes, cut in half
- 1 small tin straw mushrooms, drained
- A large handful of bean sprouts
- 1 tablespoon fish or soy sauce

HOW

- Cook the rice noodles as instructed on the packet.
- Drain the noodles and rinse with cold water.
- Heat the oil in a wok or heavy-bottomed saucepan, add the chicken and stir-fry for a few minutes until the meat is browned.
- Add the curry paste and fry for 1 minute.
- Stir in the stock and coconut milk.
- Add the tomatoes, straw mushrooms and fish or soy sauce, cover the pan and simmer over a low heat for about 20 minutes, or until the chicken is cooked.
- Place the rice noodles and bean sprouts in the bottom of a large bowl and ladle the coconut sauce over the top.

STREET STALL AUTHENTIC

Mix 1 heaped tablespoon of raw peanuts crushed with a rolling pin into the red curry paste.
Top with sliced spring onions and chopped coriander.

VEGETARIAN?

Replace the chicken with tofu or a good handful of diced mushrooms of your choice.

STIR-FRIED TREY WITH VEGETABLES

SERVES 2

A tasty Khmer fried fish speciality topped with oyster sauce veggies.

YOU NEED

- 2 tablespoons vegetable oil
- 3cm/1¼ inch ginger root, cut into matchsticks (or 1 rounded dessertspoon bottled ginger purée)
- 2 medium-thickness fish fillets
- 1 tablespoon dark soy sauce
- 1 rounded tablespoon oyster sauce
- ½ medium onion, thinly sliced
- ½ small red pepper, thinly sliced
- 1 small carrot, cut into fat matchsticks
- A small handful of basil leaves, roughly chopped

HOW

- Heat the oil in a wok or frying pan, add the ginger and cook until it starts to soften. (If using ginger purée, fry for a few seconds.)
- Add the fish and fry on both sides until golden on the outside and cooked through in the middle.
- Remove the fish from the pan and stir in the soy and oyster sauce.
- Add the vegetables and continue to stir-fry until the vegetables are soft and the sauce has reduced. (This should take about 5 minutes.)
- Return the fish to the pan, spoon the vegetables over the top, sprinkle with the chopped basil and cook for a minute or so before serving.

STREET STALL AUTHENTIC

Add a teaspoon of fish sauce at the same time as the soy and oyster sauce. **Eat** like a Cambodian. Wrap chunks of the fish in a lettuce leaf and dip into chilli sauce.

VEGETARIAN?

Replace the fish with sliced halloumi cheese or tofu and use vegetarian oyster sauce.

SNACKING IN THE NIGHT MARKETS OF LAOS

The land of gleaming Buddhist temples, parading monks and utterly unspoiled natural beauty. Trek to cascading waterfalls through timeless tribal villages, ride the rapids, or relax on one of the 'four thousand islands' of the Mekong inland delta.

After the more sophisticated sights of Vientiane and Luang Prabang things get a lot bumpier. Jam-packed bus journeys, with live chickens for companions, transport you to lush countryside and tumultuous rivers. At food stops, hawkers crowd around the bus offering a variety of creatures threaded on to sticks. Barbecued cockroaches anyone?

Laotians love wild game: in the market, jungle rodents are bargained over while croaking frogs try in vain to escape. Fortunately for the squeamish, fabulous peppery barbecued chicken, baguette sandwiches, spring rolls and spicy papaya salad are also on offer.

PING GAI: LAOTIAN CHICKEN

SERVES 2

An instant way to perk up chicken. Once the meat has been marinated, the method of cooking is quite flexible. Choose from grilling or frying, or cook in the traditional Laotian way on a barbecue.

YOU NEED

- 2 chicken breasts or legs

MARINADE

- 4 sprigs coriander, finely chopped
- 2 garlic cloves, crushed
- 1 flat teaspoon cracked black peppercorns

- 1 dessertspoon vegetable oil
- 1 dessertspoon fish or soy sauce
- 1 dessertspoon lime juice
- 1 teaspoon honey

HOW

- Mix the marinade ingredients together in a cup.
- Slash the chicken a few times on each side with a knife, lay it in a bowl and pour the marinade over the top.
- Cover the chicken with a plate and leave to marinate for 15 minutes.
- Now the choice is yours: either place the chicken under the grill, fry in a little vegetable oil or cook on a griddle or a barbecue.
- Cook both sides until nicely browned and cooked through the middle.

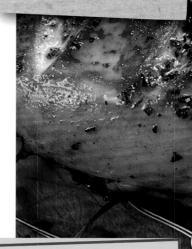

STREET STALL AUTHENTIC

Serve with spicy mango salad and sticky rice.
Add extra chopped chilli and a teaspoon of grated ginger to the mango salad.
Eat in the local way: roll the rice into small balls and dip into the spicy salad dressing.

VEGETARIAN?

Replace the chicken with thick slices of firm tofu, halloumi or paneer cheese, and use soy sauce instead of fish sauce.

MANGO SALAD

SERVES 2

In Laos green papaya salad is inseparable from grilled chicken. Green papaya is not that easy to find and can be expensive; unripe mango is a perfect substitute.

YOU NEED

- 1 small firm mango, peeled and cut into fat matchsticks
- 8 cherry tomatoes, halved
- 12 green beans, cut into 2cm/¾ inch pieces
- 110g/4oz bean sprouts
- A small handful of basil leaves, roughly chopped
- 2 tablespoons skinless natural peanuts, dry roasted in a pan and roughly chopped (optional)

DRESSING

- Juice of 1 small lime
- 1 tablespoon soy sauce
- 1 dessertspoon fish sauce (or a total of 2 tablespoons soy sauce)
- 1 teaspoon runny honey
- Sliced chilli to taste

HOW

- Whisk the dressing ingredients together in a cup. Combine the salad in a bowl, add the dressing and mix together until well coated.

THE PAGODA CAFÉS OF BAGAN, BURMA

Over a century ago Rudyard Kipling famously described Burma as 'quite unlike any land'. Experience a misty sunrise over the deserted city of Bagan or a serene sunset at the jewel-encrusted gold Shwedagon Pagoda and you will see exactly where he was coming from. Burma enchants with ancient pagodas, stunning countryside and gentle, charming people. Water babies will revel in a slow-boat journey down the Irrawaddy River or whizzing around Inle Lake in a motorized long boat, past villages on stilts and floating market gardens.

Burmese cuisine is a melting pot of Indian, Chinese and Thai: you are just as likely to lunch on curry as on stir-fried rice. The local delicacy is a salad concocted from fermented green tea leaves. It's worth giving it a go, but you probably won't be making it at home!

Shwedagon Pagoda, Burma

MOHINGAR

SERVES 2

This breakfast noodle soup might not be your first choice first thing in the morning but it makes a cracking lunch or supper.

YOU NEED

- 2 tablespoons vegetable oil
- 200g/7oz chunky fish fillets (cod, whiting or salmon)
- 75g/3oz thin vermicelli rice noodles (or 175g/6oz ready-cooked)

- ½ medium onion, grated or finely chopped
- 2 garlic cloves, grated
- 2cm/¾ inch piece ginger root, grated, or I dessertspoon bottled puréed ginger
- ½ teaspoon turmeric
- ½ teaspoon cracked black peppercorns
- 725 ml/1¼ pint fish or vegetable stock
- I lemon grass stalk, bashed with a rolling pin
- 2 heaped tablespoons tinned chickpeas, crushed until pasty
- I tablespoon fish or soy sauce

TOPPINGS
- Spring onions, sliced
- I tablespoon chopped coriander
- Lemon wedges to squeeze

HOW

- Heat I tablespoon of the oil in a frying pan and cook the fish for 3–5 minutes on each side until cooked through.
- Break the cooked fish into bite-size chunks.
- Cook the rice noodles as instructed on the packet.
- Drain the noodles and rinse with cold water, separating any that are stuck together.
- Heat the remaining oil in a wok or saucepan, add the onion, garlic and ginger and fry until brown.
- Stir in the turmeric and black pepper.
- Add the stock, lemon grass, crushed chickpeas and fish or soy sauce.
- Cover the pan and simmer the soup for 10 minutes.
- Put the noodles and flaked fish in the bottom of a bowl and spoon the hot soup over the top.
- Add toppings to taste and tuck in.

STREET STALL AUTHENTIC

Top with hard-boiled eggs cut into quarters and 2 thinly sliced garlic cloves fried in a teaspoon of vegetable oil until brown and crunchy.

VEGETARIAN?
Use diced tofu and vegetable stock.

BURMESE FRIED RICE
SERVES 2

Tea-shops in Burma are an institution. Take a low seat at one of the tiny tables, point to what looks good and soak up the local scene. Fried rice with a distinctly Chinese feel is always a safe bet.

YOU NEED

- 2 loosely packed mugs cooked rice
- 3 tablespoons vegetable oil
- 1 medium onion, thinly sliced
- 2 garlic cloves, finely chopped
- ½ teaspoon turmeric
- Ground chilli to taste
- 10 button mushrooms, cut into quarters
- 75g/3oz green beans, cut into pea-size slices
- ½ mug frozen peas, covered with boiling water and drained
- 1 dessertspoon fish or soy sauce
- 2 soft fried eggs

HOW

- Break up any clumps of rice with your (clean) fingers.
- Heat 2 tablespoons of the oil in a wok or large frying pan, add the onion and garlic and fry until soft.
- Remove half the mixture from the pan and fry the remaining half over a low-ish heat until brown and caramelized.
- Remove the brown onions from the pan and return the soft onions.
- Add the turmeric and chilli, stir-fry for a few seconds, then add the mushrooms and beans and continue to stir-fry until the vegetables are just soft.
- Add the peas and stir-fry until cooked through.
- Add the remaining oil, rice and fish or soy sauce and continue to stir-fry until the rice is steaming hot. (Add small splashes of water if the rice starts to stick.)
- Pile the stir-fried rice on plates and top with the reserved brown onions and a soft fried egg.

COOKING TIPS

Add slices of deep-fried tofu (available already fried) at the same time as the rice.

Use any type of cold leftover rice — basmati, jasmine, long grain, brown — plan ahead and cook double the quantity at suppertime the day before. Store the leftover rice in the fridge.

THE KOM CAFÉS AND NOODLE KNOCKERS OF VIETNAM

Vietnam is bursting at the seams with exciting travel experiences, its vibrant cities a hive of cool café culture and old-world charm. Watch the world speed by with a Vietnamese drip coffee, served strong with a splash of condensed milk, or join the local student crowd for a home-brewed beer at a traditional Bai hoi café (but steer clear of the menu here if dog doesn't appeal — it's often a speciality).

Hit the road and the pace slows to match rural life. Emerald-green rice paddies tended by conical-hat-wearing farmers are fringed by fairy-tale mountains, and the long coastline is strung with dazzling sights from iconic limestone islands to endless sand-dune beaches. To keep the budget in check, head to any kom café for curry and rice or enjoy a pho noodle soup. Choose the busiest-looking pho café or take a punt and stop a mobile noodle-seller.

Hanoi, Vietnam

JUNGLE CURRY

SERVES 2

A classic kom café veggie curry. Pile on top of generous scoops of boiled rice.

YOU NEED

- 2 tablespoons vegetable oil
- I small onion, thinly sliced
- 3cm/1¼ inch piece ginger root, peeled and cut into matchsticks, or I rounded dessertspoon bottled puréed ginger
- I medium carrot, cut into fat matchstick shapes
- 110g/4oz green beans, topped and tailed and cut in half
- 75g/3oz baby corn, cut in half lengthways
- ½ teaspoon turmeric
- ¼ teaspoon ground black pepper
- I small head pak choy or handful fresh spinach leaves, thinly sliced
- 110ml/4fl oz coconut milk
- Juice of ½ lime
- I dessertspoon soy sauce
- A small handful of coriander leaves, roughly chopped
- Salt

HOW

- Heat the oil in a wok or frying pan, add the onion and ginger and stir-fry until soft.
- Add the carrot, beans and baby corn, stir-fry for a couple of minutes.
- Stir in the turmeric and pepper, stir-fry for I minute.
- Add pak choy and stir-fry until the leaves start to wilt.
- Add the coconut milk, lime juice, soy sauce, coriander and a couple of tablespoons of water.
- Cover the pan and gently simmer the curry for 5 minutes or so, until the vegetables are just soft.
- Taste. If you prefer more salt, add extra to taste.

STREET STALL AUTHENTIC

Serve with a good shake of fish sauce and thinly sliced hot red chilli.

COOKING TIP

Add a handful of cooked prawns or cubed tofu at the same time as the coconut milk.

Swap green beans for mangetout or sugar-snap peas (topped and tailed and left whole).

PHO NOODLE SOUP

SERVES 2

Pho noodle soup is Vietnam in a bowl. Star anise is essential to a good pho soup. They are easy to track down in Oriental stores and most supermarkets, and keep for ages.

YOU NEED

- 110g/4oz medium flat rice noodles
- 725ml/1¼ pints beef or vegetable stock
- 2 garlic cloves, thinly sliced
- 4cm/1½ inch piece ginger root, peeled and thinly sliced
- 2 whole star anise
- 1 cinnamon stick
- A good shake of ground black pepper
- 1 tablespoon fish or soy sauce

- A small handful of sliced fresh spinach leaves
- 175g/6oz thin frying steak
- 1 tablespoon vegetable oil
- 75g/3oz bean sprouts
- 3 spring onions, thinly sliced
- 6 sprigs coriander, roughly chopped
- Thin-sliced red chilli or chilli flakes
- Salt to taste

HOW

- Cook the noodles as instructed on the packet.
- Drain the noodles and rinse with cold water, separating any that stick together.
- Pour the stock into a saucepan (with a fitted lid), add the garlic, ginger and spices and bring the pan to the boil.
- Cover the pan, reduce the heat to a minimum and simmer for 10 minutes.
- Add the fish or soy sauce and sliced spinach. When the spinach wilts, taste the soup and add extra salt if necessary.
- Season the frying steak with salt and heat the oil in a frying pan. When the oil is hot, fry the steak for 1–2 minutes on each side, until brown on the outside and a little pink on the inside. Leave the steak to sit for a few minutes before cutting into thick strips.
- Place the noodles in the bottom of a bowl, pour the hot soup over the top and top with the bean sprouts, spring onions, coriander, chilli and sliced beef or a veggie option.

STREET STALL AUTHENTIC

Top the soup with a dollop of hoisin sauce and a squeeze of lemon juice.

VEGETARIAN?

Use vegetable stock and replace the beef with sliced oyster mushrooms or Quorn meat-free 'steak' strips fried in the oil. Tofu can be either fried or added just as it comes. **Don't** miss out the star anise or the cinnamon stick. They give the soup its characteristic flavour.

INDEX OF RECIPES

WORLD STREET FOOD
EASY RECIPES FOR YOUNG TRAVELLERS

Full of simple, yet innovative, travellers' favourites, *World Street Food* is *the* cookbook for all young travellers and all beginner cooks. Carolyn and Chris Caldicott, co-founders of London's World Food Cafe, recreate the tantalizing tastes of street stalls and night markets, trattorias and tea-houses, camp-fire cook-ups and comfort food in backpacker cafes. Carolyn's recipes simplify on-the-road classics, using ingredients that you don't have to go to the ends of the earth to find and providing clear cooking instructions. Chris's stunning photographs transport you to the Mediterranean as you concoct aubergine parmigiana or piperrada sauce, to the Atacama Desert as you relish a pepper, potato and chorizo tortilla, to the heights of Table Mountain as you munch bunny chow, to a rooftop cafe overlooking the Ganges as you tuck into an easy biryani, to the pagoda cafes of Burma as you enjoy khao coconut rice noodles.

Previous books by Carolyn and Chris include *World Food Cafe*, *The Spice Routes* and *Bombay Lunchbox*.

ISBN 978-1-910258-39-2

9 781910 258392

£9.99

acorns
local children's hospice
Charity No. 700

PIMPERNEL
PRESS LTD
www.pimpernelpress.com

Price £1